THEORI
NEW WA

A TREATISE IN THE SOCIAL PSYCHOLOGY OF SCIENTIFIC THINKING IN EVERYDAY LIFE

BY ARMANDO A. ARIAS

> Familia Kummernuss
>
> I am gifting this book to you in hopes that you will develope a unique perspective on a great man, Cesar Chavez.
>
> You will come to know him in your studies of history — in this book you will come to know him as I did.
>
> I firmly believe that there is little doubt the stories in this book make a very important contribution to the reconstruction of scientific knowledge, namely, science, technology, engineering and mathematics.
>
> Winner of the International Latino Literary Award (Non-Fiction) for 2020

A publication of Somos en escrito Literary Foundation Press
Berkeley, California

> Love,
> Papa

Armando A. Arias

The Somos en escrito Literary Foundation Press is an imprint of the Somos en escrito Literary Foundation, a 501 (c) (3) organization under the IRS tax code. It is also the publisher of "Somos en escrito The Latino Literary Online Magazine," somosenescrito.com. Portions of the proceeds from sale of our books are donated to non-profit organizations of the author's and publisher's choice.

The cover painting is by Gabriella Borges, a self-taught painter and illustrator since she was a child. She attended college in San Francisco, London, and Falmouth, England, and now lives in the San Francisco Bay Area. From the author's collection.

Table of Contents

Dedication 5
Acknowledgments 7
Preface 9
SECTION 1 - SEARCHING FOR THE TRUTH 19
   Introduction 19
   Chapter One: 27
   Chapter Two: 35
   Chapter Three: 43
SECTION 2 - SCIENCE 53
   Chapter Four: 53
   Chapter Five: 61
   Chapter Six: 71
   Chapter Seven: 79
SECTION 3 - TECHNOLOGY 87
   Chapter Eight: 87
   Chapter Nine: 93
   Chapter Ten: 101
SECTION 4 - ENGINEERING 109
   Chapter Eleven: 109
   Chapter Twelve: 117
SECTION 5 - MATHEMATICS 129
   Chapter Thirteen: 129
   Chapter Fourteen: 139
   Chapter Fifteen: 149
   Chapter Sixteen: 157
SECTION 6 167
   Chapter Seventeen: 167
   Chapter Eighteen: 175
SECTION 7 - CONCLUSION 183
   Chapter Nineteen: 183
AFTERWORD 193

Armando A. Arias

Dedication

This book is dedicated to those individuals at the brink of leaping into a literary world that will transform their soul, and cause humor, originality, wondrous, and mind-bending elasticity of truth, non-truths, friction and science fiction to reinterpret relevant cultural and historical settings, so as to enhance the fluid use of different language codes, figures, symbols, events and new ways of knowing.

Armando A. Arias

Acknowledgments

Mil gracias to my wife, Patricia Arias, who supported this endeavor in so many ways I may not even be aware of – her understanding is so very deeply appreciated. Patricia is most excellent at helping me understand everyday common-sense thinking that is an attribute central both to interpreting and to translating scientific thinking.

I thank Armando Rendón for inciting a writing spirit that was asleep in me for many years.

Armando A. Arias

Preface

Most of the time, book titles aren't very telling. For instance, when you first read the title of this book, *Theorizing César Chávez*, you might think this is yet another historical biography (narrativization) of a great man revealing new details about his life; this is not by any means a new slant on an old theme. This book is not a historical chronology at all as it takes on a new tack in the form of a social psychological study of science as well as philosophical treatise, a *tractatus* about a new form of science, if you will, one that in many ways is not about the traditional views, actions and significant activities in César's life as a charismatic leader and co-founder of the United Farm Workers (UFW). Rather this book is an analysis of "what if" scenarios, as in, "What if we took César Chávez's values and beliefs and use them to theorize or to re-envision both true and meaningful fictionalized accounts in his life?" To some extent this is a treatise in turning César's values back on themselves as a method for understanding the man, embattled civic values and particularly his subconscious mind. In so doing, this allows for a method of applying his values in developing a lens to view and analyze his future Self; the Self that never was but might very well have been.

This work presents an intriguing account of how it is that César Chávez's paradigm for looking (infused with his values and beliefs) provides new intersections for the examination of the logic and reasoning behind modern day scientific thinking both as it is perceived and communicated especially to young people with little knowledge of who he was or what he stood for. This is a reflection in hopes of rousing young people and others alike to think about César Chávez in ways they never considered before. This approach has required the author to produce un-orthodox narratives that exceed the normative conventions of interpreting the life and times of César Chávez and his personal pursuit in the training of the imagination.

In so doing you will find this book at the same time riveting and perhaps stranger than fiction as the author evokes what he calls "science friction." This book intends to provide new unexplored meaning into platforms such as the national STEM (science, technology, engineering, and mathematics) program and contribute to the development of alternative practices, such as new ways of knowing science, you might even call them "lessons from a new science."

Equipped with a self-constructed César Chávez lens, the author reveals new ways of knowing and interpreting the logic of the scientific method, theoretical thinking and, in this case, new ways of knowing and interpreting science, scientific reasoning, the scientific method, and a variety of theories. The outcome is in fact a series of *lessons from a new science* grounded in empirical example after empirical example most often taken from instances and activities found in the field settings of the United Farm Workers and César's life.

This method of analysis is especially important because it gets at the way scientists communicate (or not) their research, which most often renders them ineffective to the entities that are affected by them the most, namely other researchers in related fields, students, funding agencies and the general public. This is generally the case because stake-holders remain alienated from the process and the author reveals this fact, hence, "stranger than fiction." As a strategy he begs the question that adds a unique dimension to his analysis of science: "What if César had earned a Ph.D. in science?" What would his thoughts have been on a number of topics related to such things as the science of science, methodologies used, theoretical approaches or costs of big ticket science? How might he have interpreted the goals and visions of the national STEM program? What would César's model have been for looking at modern day STEM fields and how to engage historically under-educated student populations? What would he have to say about the future of science and science in a free society? And how would he reflect on more recent scientific discoveries such as the "god particle" at the world's first super collider or landing a spacecraft on a moving comet? As a practicing scientist how might César Chávez have thought about how to engage Latinos (Chicanos/as) into science? These questions help provide the framework for this book which is meant to generate new communicational systems to describe the processes behind STEM fields and demystify them just the same.

You must first realize that the author, Dr. Sonny Boy Arias, a lover of causing *science friction* is a social psychologist by trade, storyteller at heart, and radiant writer who promotes a sparkling interchange of ideas that expands the scientific imagination, chooses to dismantle parts of the scientific method, and lift the veil of objectivity through what may very well have been César's view. Sonny Boy's methods for doing so utilize Carl Jung's (famed Swiss psychotherapist) concept of "individuation," the:

> *Psychological process of integrating the opposites including the conscious with the unconscious, while still maintaining their relative autonomy.*

It is through *individuation* as the central process of his human development that we come to understand the depths of César Chávez through the fictitious lens the author develops predicated on César's values, beliefs and visions, thus the advent of his *science friction*. To be sure the César Chávez presented is fictional, the character in this book, and Dr. Sonny Boy is in fact his creator. Sonny Boy is no doubt a walking contradiction himself divided by the existence of his Sonny Boy Self (the storyteller) and that of Dr. Sonny Boy, the social psychologist who researches the methodologies (bench work) of a variety of scientists. Divided as his Self's (in a social psychological sense) may be Dr. Sonny Boy finds in his new *personification* (Jung) the voice of Sonny Boy, a storyteller who writes under the general rubric *of historias verdaderas mentiras autenticas – true stories and authentic lies*. Why? You might ask. Because it gives each chapter a unique feel while in search of a way for promoting the intensification of cross-disciplinary relations between stocks of knowledge in turn producing a more functional relationship between such entities.

Moreover, the author presents lessons in a new science and new ways of knowing traditional STEM fields of study: science, technology, engineering and mathematics, but also within the social and psychological contradictions of three Self's he presents in César Chávez: a young César, a César at the time of his death, and an older César with a Ph.D. in science whom we never got to know.

"Three Césars" early sketch by Gabriella Borges

Sonny Boy says in a personal revelation that "he heard from César Chávez" (following his untimely death), who encouraged him to create a "theory of theorizing" by infusing his (César's) values and beliefs as the overlay of a new paradigm for examining and analyzing science (especially, scientific methods). Sonny Boy loves to cause confusion, contradictions and crosswinds in forging ideas between the arts, humanities, social and behavioral and hard sciences; this is why the idea of theorizing César Chávez is so intriguing as this approach to idea development will no doubt be found as original, visionary and inspiring. In constant search for techniques to train the imagination, Sonny Boy brings in his approach to *science friction* a presence to the absence of César Chávez. To some extent, the book is meant to provide a vision for alternate bottom-up approaches unlike top-down ways of knowing traditional science. It is what he calls an "inoculation against bad science." At the same time Sonny Boy's ideas can be found to be most hilarious, terrifying, surreal, and at the same time his fictionalized accounts can seem real, really-real. This process is the ability to dream his ideas into being; besides, Sonny Boy is Sonny Boy and everybody else is everybody else.

In an attempt to stir the imagination, this book is a radical preconception of the life of César Chávez. It gives the book a unique quality and feel, while at the same time it is meant to reassert César's relevance (especially to future generations). It is also meant to move beyond traditional historical interpretations of his life and induce a new way of knowing him, through new intersections for the examination of the sciences. By introducing visionary travails, Sonny Boy takes great liberties with his own imagination by introducing César to his future Self (in a social psychological sense): hence, the act of "theorizing César Chávez." In so doing Sonny Boy creates a lens allowing him critically to examine the state of science, namely, scientific strategies and reasoning and the uncertainty about truth and truth seeking, something César found curiouser and curiouser throughout his life. Sonny Boy is much like César Chávez as he marries uncertainty about the truth and can see it no other way, and like César sees propitious signs that science can change the way we live and the manner in which we relate to one another and also that science by its very nature is an ambiguous enterprise.

Sonny Boy demonstrates how César's logic and view of everyday phenomena coincide with the process of the scientific method, the logic, strategies and approaches to his (César's) bench work is very similar to that of a hard scientist. He is not suggesting that César took it upon himself to learn the particulars of science at an advanced level, even though he was in fact somewhat autodidactic (a lifelong self-learner) he had the uncanny ability to feel the future and in so doing (as evidenced by this work) caused us to have to expand our imagination. Rather, Sonny Boy is more than just suggesting that César's paradigm for viewing everyday life is similar to the systematic logic one uses when applying the scientific method; there is after all logic to everything and logic often takes the form of theory. César's skepticism for example kept him searching for the truth while always questioning authority – this was his nature, so, too, were his strong feelings for ideas most particularly related to injustices and related unintentional outcomes once realized. Although never officially diagnosed, psychoanalysts observed synesthesia as part of César's human condition which gave him the uncanny ability to link ideas (especially across and between disciplines) most people would see as un-linkable. Synesthesia is a cognitive condition in humans that supports a superlative logic that most people will never experience; this is what led to his ability to think out-of-the-box in ways most could not imagine. Thus, he didn't just question authority; he questioned everything. He even questioned the authority of authority, just as he questioned his own authoritative existence. The analogy found in science would be that say "Dr. César Chávez," the scientist, would by virtue of his values and beliefs question existing paradigms through critical examination of the methods applied at the bench work of scientists as well as the theoretical approaches they chose (all assumed under an existing paradigm). Even though scientists carry this idea around in their heads in daily life, the act of questioning the existing paradigm in one's research (publications, lectures or presentations at professional meetings, etc.) is something very rare in the scientific community, with the exception of those very few scientists who actually cause true scientific revolutions leading to paradigm shifts; yet for "Dr. César Chávez," the hard scientist, this would be a starting point of departure. Freud might say of Dr. Chavez and of all truly truth- seeking scientists:

> *Your god shows you something you can't have is just out of reach and keeps you wanting it for a lifetime, and that is the meaning of your life!*

Philosophically, this is why you may find this work stranger than fiction as no one has performed an analysis of César Chávez in this way until now. It didn't matter what situation (like avoiding physical altercations with farmers), César always thought-up a solution that was out-of-the-box to keep people safe, like drawing farm workers out of the fields (located on private property) with a makeshift altar (dedicated to the Virgin Mary) he and his brother mounted on the back of a flatbed truck. He more than understood that the situatedness of any situation was more about the process than the goal, like during the Delano grape strike he would say, "It's not about the grapes, it's about the people!"

César was especially curious that scientists always seemed to be changing their view of whatever it was they were researching (especially in lab-like situations). For César the journey in science consisted of the methods scientists use or the sequential step-by-step process they employed in their bench work, plus he often drew analogies to how the imagination can be spurred at the scientist's bench and in the farm worker while toiling in the fields.

The idea to theorize César Chávez came to Sonny Boy in the form of a loud voice from the Heavens of Aztlan (a not so mythical place) directly from César not long after his passing:

When César came to Sonny Boy in this way he thought, "How César Chávez of you, César Chávez, to respond with such an out-of-the-box idea! Whoa!" As a direct result, Sonny Boy had a re-occurring dream in which César kept saying to him:

Theorize me, Sonny Boy, theorize me!

In theorizing César Chávez, Sonny Boy takes great liberties in taking what he knows of César's thoughts, ideas, world view and self and psychoanalyzes them all against the backdrop of reinterpreting our assumptions about science and most of all focusing on the training of the imagination. Sonny Boy is a genius inasmuch as he both creates and captures César's novel theory of scientific logic. Historians use the term "subjunctive history" to describe a historical analysis that creates both an *irrealis* and *realis* mood indicative of a practice in search of methods for explaining the truth. In this book, Sonny Boy employs a similar practice and stresses that in theorizing César Chávez he had to be at times hypothetical and counterfactual. Moreover, *Theorizing César Chávez* is not meant to be a historical recount of the life and times of this great man; it is rather meant to be a new and futuristic account, one that didn't happen, but if it had may have turned out this way. Recounting César's life is not the goal of the book; the goal is to infuse César's values into existing ways of knowing and experiencing scientific inquiry: its methods (bench work), theories (postulates and what they stand for), and contradictions in order to derive new intersections for understanding scientific criticism and to some extent reveal the larger anxiety about the nature and role of science in American society. Sonny Boy takes a brilliant leap of faith and in so doing creates lessons in a new science.

In *Theorizing Cesar Chavez*, Sonny Boy sheds new light not only on the mind of César Chávez but also on overarching perennial problems in science, scientific method, scientific theory as well as scientific discovery and the nature of paradigm shifts. Again, in so doing what follows are observations César may have made on the national STEM program and on some problems the STEM program does not know it has, especially in terms of serving underrepresented populations, such as Latinos.

Giving a scientific intellectual voice to César Chávez within a popular vernacular (scientific speak infused with some street talk and concepts that are easy to understand), Sonny Boy writes with spellbinding intelligence while taking great liberties in the social construction of a personification in "Dr. César Chávez" as the comparative future Self (had he lived on) in hopes of shedding new light on existing topics of scientific inquiry and in providing new interpretations for what he stood for and how this may lead to solving problems in science (STEM fields). For both César Chávez and Sonny Boy this work serves as a social historical memoir of a sort and an uncanny reminder that we should always question the truth and not live a duality of realities filled with truths, non-truths and unspeakable truths.

Until now César's ideas, thoughts and thinking process have not been psychoanalyzed against the backdrop of science nor have they been viewed from early formation to later in his life as they have in *Theorizing César Chávez*. His influence is viewed historically as a charismatic individual with strong values always in search of solutions for problems between farmers and farm workers. Until now, these ideas have not been dissected for intellectual interpretation. Sonny Boy is the first to admit, he is not a scholar of the life, times and/or history of César Chávez but he adds:

> *I did ask him if I could look deeply into his eyes, and I did and he was in there, I walked with him, I held his hand in Watsonville at a picket against exploitative practices of strawberry farmers, we shared a quesadilla, I breathed his breath at a crucial time, I sang De Colores within earshot, I stood shoulder-to-shoulder with him and felt his soul while trying to think his thoughts and this work is a partial view of what I felt, sensed and experienced in this great man. I won't forget the last thing he told me: "Time marches on Dr. Sonny Boy and we have to keep pace a la brava."*

Que viva César Chávez y que viva Sonny Boy!

Joaquin Emiliano Inzunza
Nobel Prize in Particle Physics

SECTION 1 - SEARCHING FOR THE TRUTH

Introduction

To Know César Chávez is to Know His Greatest Challenge: Searching for the Truth

If you really want to know César Chávez, consider an examination of his ideas, thoughts and actions, and how these are integrated in such a manner as to question the truth about any phenomenon. Basically, he found human behavior, as he would say, "peculiarly interesting." Many books have been written about his life, most are a historical chronicle of his actions and activities within the United Farm Workers (UFW) and how these caused social change in American society at the same time impacting the shaping and/or reshaping of policies, rules and laws pertaining to farm worker labor.

Two of the most well documented accounts of César's life are Miriam Pawel's *The Crusades of César Chávez*, (Bloomsbury Press, 2014) and Richard Griswold Del Castillo's *César Chávez: A Triumph of Spirit* (Oklahoma Press, 1995). To be sure in both cases they each capture who he was and what he stood for. What they don't capture is the essence of his heart, soul and inner-Self (in a social psychological sense) as this work aims to do, that is, provide a clear understanding of the life choices César Chávez made, predicated on how he socially constructed his reality in everyday life that have until now remained a mystery.

In this work I'm certainly not suggesting that we revisit and cross-fact-check existing books and other materials documenting the plight of the United Farm Workers for it is important to leave that work up to experts like Pawel and Griswold Del Castillo whose training in history and in writing it is to do so. Unlike any analysis of César Chávez to date, I'm suggesting a completely different vantage point: a focus on his mind: ideas, thoughts, as well as idiosyncratic feelings to the level of subjective consciousness a social psychological focus on the manner in which he constructs his reality in everyday life if you will. Speaking from a social psychological school of thought, my goal in this work is to peel back whatever layers of his reality we can in the life of this great yet complex man and reveal new insights into César's innermost Self. The analogy to what I am saying is to view all of the works that have ever been written about César like someone you have known for many years and suddenly through this work (an analysis of his cognitive processes) discover that you never really knew much about him.

To some extent this is a study of César's cognitive processes and consciousness. I realize that only he could reflect on that aspect of capturing his reality and I know his perspective on this would be rather existential, as he once put it:

> *No one knows my experiences, thoughts, actions, likes, dislikes and feelings better than I, yet I am even a stranger to myself.*

In this work I want to share some ways to think about how César ordered his mind, recognizable by his indexical expressions as found in his superlative logic, his philosophy and continuous ability to think outside-the-box. I especially want to shed light on his search for the *truth*, the *absolute truth*, about various phenomena that captured his imagination; after all, it was creativity that captured him. Moreover, I will infuse his philosophy to elevate oppressed people, his quest and vision for social change as well as his love for education through examination of the *patterns of his objectifications*. An example of this is how César in his personal philosophy would often objectify something by rethinking its possible realities. For instance, he would often say:

> *In the absence of the United Farm Workers Union, we would have to create one.*

This serves as a starting point to understand how speaking from his philosophical-logical point of view, what he means is that there has always been a need for an organization like the UFW because the problem of exploitation has been around since the beginning of humanity—and in this case, farmworkers in the U.S. never organized until the UFW was created; it's the latter part of his logic that makes his philosophy, superlative. To be sure the average person on the street nor the farm worker may never ponder such a postulate on their own accord--it was a logic he found as an effective tool to get people thinking differently and attract them to the plight of farm workers. Again, his logic helped him communicate to people in daily life the austere working conditions in which farm workers toiled in daily life. Frankly speaking, before César came around farm workers didn't see themselves as a marginalized group; they were only interested in earning a wage at most any cost. At a fireside chat with one of the most influential thinkers of our time, the noted social philosopher, Herbert Marcuse, once observed this about César's thinking:

> *In his plight to assist farmworkers, his thinking demands abstraction from the painful world of their human condition.*

César's search for the truth was essentially on behalf of the common man and he (like Socrates) needed to first search for and understand the *concept* of truth.

Very much like a modern day scientist César was always in search of better tools for communicating his ideas and he always felt he needed more educational training to do so. Said differently, for César it didn't matter if what he said was an absolute fact; what was important to him was the outcome--organizing the UFW while at the same time exposing the exploitative tactics of farm owners. So that even when he would say to people that "education was important," he was truly minimizing his personal meaning of the word "education" as it had a deep and profound impact on him over the course of his life in ways we can identify and analyze. César would use the word "education" rather than "knowledge" because he realized it was effective; he found himself using the old adage *"knowledge is power"* because he knew this is what people wanted to hear.

For César, *knowledge* could be garnered from anywhere and anything and he found this idea (the one that stirred him the most) too complicated to try to describe even more so to large public audiences. He also felt he didn't possess the training in rhetoric to properly present ideas (simple and/or complex) a characteristic that took up a good deal of his time when reflecting but it never stopped him from trying to improve upon that characteristic. Think about what he was up against in this way: how could he possibly get philosophical with a large public audience and at the same time move them to action. Fred Ross encouraged César to have his dog, "Huelga," ("strike" as in, to go on strike) on stage with him by his side during especially large public appearances as he was training the dog to bark upon signaling him from the audience. Interestingly enough audiences often cheered when Huelga would bark and they would respond with "Si se puede!" ("Yes we can!). Once during one of César's speeches, Huelga darted off the stage after a cat and César commented in the microphone for all to hear "Huelga has gone on strike!" Hearing this the crowd went wild with laughter. César admits it was one of the biggest laughs of his life; it was also at the peak of his activism and the laughter really helped everyone let off some steam. César enjoyed making jokes and this helped him objectify ideas that were somehow hard to communicate yet not fully understood. The idea of Huelga going on strike was indicative of clear communication. It was also clear that even though he and Huelga had an understanding, Huelga was going to do what he wanted to do.

César's Novel Theory of Scientific Logic: The Truth in Absolute Truth is Fiction

It's one thing to objectify the idea of labor organizing, it's another to objectify the idea of how César saw everything as *fiction* (objectifying everything) and he knew it was too difficult to communicate in his speeches. Even so he would sometimes run the risk of introducing a complex idea (like how there is no absolute truth) that required a more intimate setting for further dialog and it never worked. When César interjected philosophical ideas into his speeches significant others in the UFW like Doña Dolores Huerta would give him *mal ojo* (stink-eye) and/or Phil Esparza co-founder of the *Teatro Campesino* would put on a skeleton mask and walk in front of the stage, it took tactics like these to remind him. At times César would become too emotional and it was too difficult to stick with the speech outlined before him; Socrates had the very same response or that the emotional drive would overtake what was written in the speech and so he most often spoke from the heart.

His thinking in this example was at a philosophical level Herbert Marcuse's interpretation was that for César:

> *Whatever the given reality [of the UFW] was, it is not the real thing!*

At the same time from an intellectual perspective, he was interested in how it is that in one sentence in one single moment he could begin to change the minds of men and women, just as Doña Dolores Huerta had when she first uttered the words "Si se puede!" ("Yes we can!"): he knew the power of simple yet powerful rhetoric. For César the truth about the powerful saying, "Si se puede!" became the scrub brush for cleaning up a dirty society, which he saw driven by greed. It becomes all at once *Marcusesque*. He also loved Alberto Einstein's saying, "Keep it simple, but not too simple." César knew people saw him as a leader, labor organizer, charismatic individual, fearless of standing up to big agribusiness, and so to a large extent he had to sustain the public image as he started down the pathway to self-discovery.

In this book I take the liberty of "theorizing" César Chávez while at the same time promoting the "marriage" of the arts, humanities, social and behavioral and hard sciences in anticipation of the needs and trends in a continuously evolving society striving to remain at the top of scientific discovery on the world stage, especially in the STEM fields: science, technology, engineering and mathematics. The creation of the

STEM program as a national initiative is solid evidence that American society is directly addressing our need to improve upon scientific discovery in this nation. By looking through *César's lens* (his paradigm for looking) this becomes a method for awakening our creativity by sparking curiosity through his insights.

César's natural way of thinking, his way of socially constructing his reality, afforded him the ability to think of things, like solutions to problems he was confronted with, as an activist and social change artist often faced with having to come up with solutions on the spot. Hundreds, sometimes thousands, of people were often literally waiting for his response (solution) in situations during a strike and waited eagerly for his response, whereas for most of us, we would take much more time and have to grapple with numerous ideas in search of solutions to the self-same issues. It would be difficult to disagree with him in regard to major issues inasmuch as exploitation, for instance, has been around for thousands of years; it just took the right time in history and the right charismatic character in him to provide new interpretations to unveil it and its objectivity. In one way this captures the paradox of César's paradigm for looking that many people enjoyed but never recognized. A related idea would be to think that before César came around farm workers didn't see themselves as a marginalized group. Many of them were from Mexico and they didn't see themselves that way in their *Patria* (Mother land) and this is what they carried around in their heads. Farm workers were busy simply trying to make a living by moving from one unstable situation to another, all the while being exploited at every turn; few members of American society could endure such an existence.

In his epic book, *One-Dimensional Man: Studies in the Ideology of Advanced Industrial Society* (Beacon Press, 1964), Herbert Marcuse would view farm workers as a people not yet "objectified," hence, it wasn't until they could come to see themselves as something other than farmworkers or as a class of marginalized people that they could break from "one dimensional" thinking and rise up and organize and this is what César helped them to see. One could argue that even today as the efforts of the United Farm Workers have waxed and waned, farm workers are experiencing high degrees of alienation from their Self's (in a social psychological sense), from their family members (both nuclear and extended), their communities and from American society; at least César's actions gave them something to think about and that alone helped stem some forms of alienation.

Moreover, Marcuse's point is that in helping farm workers come to see themselves as other people, especially intellectuals, saw them, namely as an "oppressed, exploited class, and modern day slaves," by objectifying them in this way César was a man in search of solutions grounding (providing real life solutions) to the paradoxical meanings of his own creation. In many ways what César really led was a symbolic crusade for the development of "social goods" and used the idea to create networks of progressive change—this is what is meant by his finding solutions to problems farm workers didn't know they had; hence, they really didn't think much about being an oppressed class of people as they were more focused on getting a job and earning enough money to return to their *Patria (Mother Land)*. As an activist César developed strategies for collaborating with others, he gathered data, put facts together and provided the foresight and energy, while taking action to make a real difference in addressing major problems facing farm workers (as well as other oppressed classes) in American society. In so doing, his personal plight became that of bringing attention to others in similar situations throughout the world; his span of thinking varied from austere living and working conditions to environmental sustainability issues. One is left with the indelible impression that César more than sensed the relationship between ideology and the advancements in the American industrialized society. He was both living and transforming himself away from existing as Marcuse's *One Dimensional Man*.

It's no wonder César came to see Marcuse's book, *One Dimensional Man*, as a training manual for social activism and that the idea that caused him great consternation in daily life was the idea of the *truth* and its relation to *absolute truth*. He found the nature of searching for the truth just as captivating as any passionate scientist. It didn't matter if it were something that caught his attention in the daily news or hearing about a new theory about global warming; he used to say, "Theories are all fiction!" As an example, what really got his goat about the topic of global warming was that he was aware that there are thousands of environmental scientists that have devoted their careers to the study of this topic, yet for political reasons their scientific perspective is reduced to that of the average person on the street who only knows what they hear on the radio or have learned from what is reported on the television. When he spoke at the Kennedy School at Harvard University in 1992, he, like Howard Zinn focused on how boycotts are more effective than voting, he stressed that Harvard ought not to be serving grapes and that everyone should be boycotting grapes, and he presented the perils of using pesticides within the context of the thinning of the uterus wall (a point in his speech that really caught the attention of the audience), He knew that within American society, "perception is everything." César connected people to positive experiences when he spoke and in the actions he took. It was this sort of strategic vision that helped him communicate ideas.

Chapter One:

Capturing César's Search for the Truth

When César was most active people talked to him about writing a book about himself and the United Farm Workers. This caused him a good deal of consternation, not because he didn't think they could do a good job but rather he didn't know if they could hold people's imaginations. In 1990, César enjoyed talking to Ricardo Griswold del Castillo, a history professor at San Diego State University, about his book project and once commented tongue-in-cheek:

> *Ricardo, your manuscript is so detailed even I do not recall the details of your detailed descriptions.*

The conversation that ensued between César and Ricardo ended with César's wish to add a prolegomena to his book, *Cesar Chavez: The Struggle for Justice/La Lucha Por La Justicia* by Richard Griswold Del Castillo, published in 2008 by Piñata Books (first published in 2002). César knew that even great writers like Ricardo would never truly capture the truth, "How could they capture the truth?" he would ask. "They weren't at the event they are writing about?" Ricardo tried explaining the methods historians used but just like scientists from competing paradigms César had a paradigm for describing events different from that of most modern day historians; that isn't to say he knew historians could chronicle events, he just felt there was a lot more to what happened during times of social protest than could be truly captured in a book. One of César's greatest personal consternations was that writers certainly weren't going to capture what was going on in his head, his ideas, thoughts and feelings. He didn't want to be depicted as a "Poor boy done good!" apologetic, or even as the great confessor. He came to the realization that what he wanted more than anything has been glossed over in the many books about his life, that is, the meaning of his inner Self (in a social psychological sense).

Even while he was alive César knew people were not writing about him, rather they were writing about his actions and interactions with others, he was after all undergoing personal transformations that were deep and he had not reached a point in his transformation that could emerge as a new sense of self in a society all at once both rejecting and accepting his ideas. César's analogy to this he often expressed in this way:

> *I went to the doctor who showed me an X-ray of my chest, he then turned to me and said, 'This is a picture of the real you!' The doctor didn't know how further from the truth he could be this was hardly a picture of the real me!*

César didn't take issue with the physician at the time as his comment sent him in a downward direction, a hermeneutic spiral if you will, raising many more questions about the meaning of his life and the meaning of life for others. César's point was that the X-ray was for him an image (a rather poor image) of his flesh and bones; it did not capture his heart, soul or self, again, in his own opinion, "It was hardly a picture of the real César Chávez!" To draw this analogy even further, for César any books written about himself or of the United Farm Workers were simply an X-ray capturing a seemingly mirrored-image of the truth, but not capturing the absolute truth only found in his heart, soul and self. Anything written about him or the United Farm Workers was simply someone's biased perspective—this was his point to Ricardo Griswold Del Castillo:

> *The work of historians may be well documented but it is only a perspective and that's what makes it fiction, so in reality history is actually fiction based on fiction.*

When psychoanalyzing his ideas, thoughts and actions in this work, this is a point we cannot take lightly because it was central to his paradigm for looking at everyday life. César had been a party to many social protest moments and activities captured and reported by the news media that were never depicted in the manner in which he experienced them, never! César liked to give the example that in the 1965 infamous March from Delano (to Sacramento), in one day he heard that up to a 1,000 people had joined him, so he asked Fred Ross his lead organizer at the time to count. When Fred returned some two hours later he said there were thousands of people and that he couldn't count because people were joining the march along the way. Much like a hard scientist or even a statistician, César became preoccupied at times with the idea of incommensurability or that some things are not countable. He often chastised reports in the newspapers or radio from the U.S. Census or the U.S. Immigration Services. Case in point: he knew many people that came across the U.S. – Mexico border repeatedly and surreptitiously without being included in the numbers of "illegal immigrants" that were being reported; for him science remained ex post facto. His point is well-taken. It's a perspective that would eat at his psyche because he saw change in everything, especially when it came to numbers and people. César said that when his son turned three years of age he asked him "How many stars are there in the sky?" and his son replied "seven". It struck César that it really didn't matter how many stars there are in the sky seven or a billion, we will never be able to count them, just like undocumented Mexicans who traverse back-and-forth across the U.S. – Mexico border, and are never apprehended. The fact that he became "star-struck" over various phenomena introduces us to his thinking process which is, in a manner of analysis, parallel to that of scientists. This is what has struck me about applying his thought processes as a means of evaluating scientific validity evidenced by the examples and case-study issues I raise in this work.

It is for this and similar reasons that in an attempt to get at the truth of any phenomenon I take César Chávez's perspective and use fictionalized accounts and at the same time claim that they are perhaps the truest accounts possible, yet deemed "fictional" in a fact-checking world. Again, his message to historians and academics alike was that the truth they conveyed as factual could only in fact be fictional. César's logic was philosophical and superlative indeed. He said he wanted to create a bumper sticker with this saying on it:

The only truth is a fictionalized account of the truth!

Using this logic this work is an attempt to apply César's logic on itself; it's a style I heard a historian (unknown) call "subjunctive history." Using César's logic, however, I create a way to report true incidents, interactions and situations in a type of rhetoric of historias verdaderas mentiras auténticas or true stories and authentic lies, similar in fashion to how historians often embellish the truth. So when people asked César if they could write a book about him, it caused him some consternation not because he didn't believe in their ability to do so, but because he knew that whatever they produced would not capture the logic of getting at the absolute truth the way he experienced it and/or felt it; he was struggling with how to communicate this idea and this problematic captured his imagination his entire life. He felt it was very important for someone to capture what was in his heart; he also knew it was impossible to explain what was in his heart as he grappled with it every day. In his later years he believed that it was important to discover one's consciousness in order to get at who people really were. I don't think more than a handful of people realized this about César. In an attempt to sooth his thinking somewhat I once shared with him what the philosopher Ludwig Wittgenstein said:

Someone who knows too much finds it hard not to lie.

I have to tell you César sought refuge in that saying. We never talked about what refuge he found in the saying, but I could tell it tickled him inasmuch as it was within the realm of his thinking about the truth. The saying certainly captured his feeling about scientists as he wanted to trust them but wasn't sure they could trust themselves. It's like the time César's father was scrambling to gather the finances to save their home from foreclosure. César heard his father ask his uncle to invest in the house and said to him "Don't worry about the money, you can trust me!" Hearing this César became even more worried because he wasn't sure his father could ever pay back his uncle even if it did save the house from foreclosure. In other words, he may have trusted his father but he didn't necessarily trust his financial judgment, especially when it came to finances and this caused a state of mind of constant contradictions.

In his classic book, *The Structure of Scientific Revolutions* (University of Chicago Press, 1962), Thomas Kuhn presents a very similar logic about how it is that scientific revolutions and paradigm shifts occur. It's a superlative logic much like that of César Chávez, except Kuhn points to the development of paradigms (widely accepted models) in the same fashion as César talks about fiction. When it comes to searching for the truth about anything at all they both would agree, "Everything is perceived from a biased point of view."

They were certainly both logical positivists concerned with the notion of *objectivity* as well as the veil of objectivity. Kuhn falls short of referring to science as "fiction" because if he did scientists would not take him seriously, hence, for political reasons tied to the manner in which Western science is discussed, a rhetoric is expected when describing the scientific methods utilized by modern day scientists. To speak outside that rubric would deem one such as Kuhn not to be taken seriously. César would see it as "another one of those sweeping it under the rug" *movidas* (moves with a political intent), allowing them to move their work forward in the absence of facts that are absolute; it's similar to Adam Smith's notion of the "invisible hand" in socio-economics—people often make financial moves that most people will never see and/or understand. The idea is that you can move past something simply because we agree to allow ourselves to do so. It's the unspeakable truth about something "everybody knows but nobody talks about."

Conversely, César can use the word "fiction" as a communication device because he is addressing an audience open to searching for new solutions to social problems predicated on a natural drive to change the human condition; the power behind such a drive allows for more open-mindedness in situations such as these. It doesn't work that way in science, however, as some hard scientists will often fact check new ideas to the point of absurdity, rendering the scientific imagination useless because fact checking can go on forever, never revealing the truth or meaning of the human experience. They produce a methodology for going backwards, as suggested by the French phenomenological philosopher, Maurice Merleau-Ponty in his book, *Le Visible et L'Invisible* (The Visible and the Invisible, Alphonso Lingis translator, Evanston: Northwestern University Press, 1968). The very act of making insightful connections between fiction and non-fiction is precisely what scientists do; it is the "magic" all scientists try to create in search of a moment of insight that may lead to a scientific breakthrough. Why do you think experts like physicists are called in on a routine basis to provide advice on Hollywood science fiction movies? This is why I am convinced that had César been trained as a physicist, he would have joined the ranks of Alberto Einstein.

Much like César, Kuhn was causing quite a stir in his respective field arguing that "scientific fields undergo periodic 'paradigm shifts,'" which I see as very similar to César's quest to help people, especially in social protest movements, realize that nonviolent social change is possible. Think about it this way, both Kuhn and César *were* breaking new ground, presenting new ideas that were deeply influential, each was causing a paradigm shift in their areas, their ideas, thoughts and actions that influenced people to try new approaches within the realm of their own craft. As Kuhn (1962) would put it:

> *When the paradigm is successful, the profession will have solved problems that its members could scarcely have imagined and would never have undertaken without commitment to the paradigm.*

César was an excellent puzzle-solver and in so doing was successful at presenting an expanded paradigm (surrounding the exploitative practices of farmers) by puzzle-solving issues related to the oppression of peoples on a global basis. By all accounts he was especially good at identifying solutions to problems people didn't know they had. This strategy coupled with the UFW saying, "Si se puede" (Yes we can!)," provided a productive platform for a paradigm shift during the early 1960s. In short, it was time for the exploitative practices of the farmers to be exposed and for people to react, and react they did. The same process occurs in scientific discovery. Scientists more often than not locate solutions to problems that only present themselves as doubtful of any solution whatsoever, until such time as a solution is matched with a perceived problem. Kuhn's overarching point is that this is all "normal science" and even though it causes teams of scientists to become very productive, César remained quite cautious about this reality as in his eyes it lacks the profundity of the reality.

The early 1960s weren't just revolutionary for American societal change; from a social movement perspective it was heralding a time for scientific breakthroughs in science as well, César providing the lead in societal transformation and social change and Kuhn providing leadership in rethinking the nature of scientific revolutions. The superlative logic of both these men caused in many ways a "marriage" of street smarts and scientific knowledge if you will as they were both fascinated by comparing truth and *absolute truth* and preoccupied with the idea of *incommensurability* or that things can't really be counted. Kuhn, in his capacity as a physicist, was conflicted over the National Science Foundation's ten billion dollar grant in support of the world's first super collider project in Waxahachie, Texas, as he truly believed that with proper instrumentation *particles* (in the physicists' sense) can continually be split. César had a similar belief when it came to human behavior as he came to believe that human consciousness could be peeled back layer-after-layer with an endless amount of discovery waiting to be revealed.

The link between the scientific thinking behind these two men is not far-fetched at all. The way I see it, we are moving from street smarts in César's thinking to scientific knowledge in Kuhn's thinking and back again. After all, it was Descartes who argued from a common sense point of view that street smarts form the basis to scientific knowledge and that we have simply gone away from that idea; hence, we should not forget, as Socrates states, "All knowledge stems from one book." [Note: In this light the American Chemical Society in its attempt to become more cross-disciplinary ought to provide César Chávez with the Thomas Kuhn Paradigm Shift Award because it is awarded to people "who present original views that are at odds with mainstream scientific understanding. The winner is selected based on the novelty of the viewpoint and its potential impact if it were to be widely accepted."]

This book provides an abundance of evidence in this regard. ¡Que viva César Chávez!

Concomitantly, there is much to be said about the similarities in thought between Kuhn and Chávez in Kuhn's book, *The Essential Tension: Selected Studies in Scientific Tradition and Change,* (Chicago and London: University of Chicago Press, 1977). Kuhn addresses an entire litany of scientific concepts that can be applied in the world of the social sciences, such as: social change, essential tension, tradition, conflict, change agents, and more. Fact is, the similarities and the manner in which they apply to human behavior are uncanny. Kuhn would have certainly found this to be the case had he interviewed César the way he had Niels Bohr, Leon Rosenfeld and Aage Peterson in order to gain insight into their thinking. Making connections of this sort started at an early age for César and this is what captured his imagination throughout his life; for him interdisciplinary as well as cross-disciplinary thinking are paramount.

César's ideas and thoughts relative to Western science would not be taken seriously, however, because he had no formal training in science and/or the scientific method yet, in truth, he possessed much of the scientific logic employed in his own street smarts—this is what I refer to as his superlative logic.

Chapter Two:

The Eighth Grade

César can seem to be telling us what to think, and at the same time be one who is not suggesting ideas at all, letting others speak for themselves. In other words, he often drew together adages, labels and symbols as a means of understanding the world around him, a revelation of his own palpability.

César often reflected on the two small all-white plaster busts located at the front of his eighth grade classroom, one of Socrates and one of Plato. He said that at times his teacher, Mrs. Tobias, would hold them up and quote one of them. She stressed that Socrates was the most intelligent man that ever lived. César was so struck by that thought that he never outlived the idea. He used to think, "How could one man be the most intelligent man ever?"

By the end of his eighth grade year he was convinced that Plato made more sense than Socrates and Plato was Socrates' student. The quote that Mrs. Tobias repeated the most was when Socrates suggests, "Know thyself." It was an idea that César took to heart, because he felt strongly about being true to himself and to his Self (in a social psychological sense). Being true to himself was something he says he picked up from his mother as she always told him to never lie and he took this to mean to never ever lie to himself as this would be a sin and he would never feel good about himself. One thing for sure was that he felt different than most people with his ethnic background; he felt more like he was a "citizen of the world." He didn't know why he felt this way, he just did.

At the height of César's labor organizing efforts in the 1960s, the term "Hispanic" had not yet been popularized in American society (the term had not yet been conceived by the White male statistician in the U.S. Census Bureau who came up with the term in hopes of creating a category for all Latinos to choose and make his job easier) and due to the political activities being carried out by Chicanos (who they themselves were organizing for social change). Our society had not yet made distinctions between such labels as "Hispanics," "Latinos," "Mexican-Americans," "Spanish," or "Chicanos." Many Latino groups make note that historically they were subjected to abuses by the Spanish.

No matter how many people labelled themselves "Spanish," people were coming to the realization that there was a need for demonstrative social change in this country and César Chávez's labor organizing efforts as well as Chicano protest activities provided direct evidence of this. His eighth grade teacher was a self-proclaimed Pilgrim and he observed how much she would apologize to the class for what "her people" had done to past relatives of "our people." What César took away from this was not so much the experience of how people may have labelled him, rather how he experienced life in collaboration with people. He could see that Mrs. Tobias was uncomfortable in her Pilgrim skin. He responded more to the stronger ideas about how change was the one thing we all knew was going to happen and then she would quote Socrates:

> *The secret of change is to focus all of your energy, not on fighting the old, but on building the new.*

Her advice or that of Socrates rang true to his ears.

In recognition of Thanksgiving Day, Mrs. Tobias brought buttermilk to César's eighth grade class and asked him to churn it with an old time wooden device "much like the Pilgrims used to do." The more César churned the faster his strokes and the faster his strokes the more the other students urged him on and the more Mrs. Tobias told him to focus his energy. César admitted that the task was arduous but that he gladly complied because he trusted her. After several minutes she had him stop, lifted the lid on the old wooden device and down at the bottom was a clump of butter. All of his 14 classmates were in awe at this and as César puts it:

They thought it was magic or that I had special powers and they treated me different till the end of the school year.

    At that very moment he felt that it wasn't about the butter or even the fact that he liked Mrs. Tobias because she treated him and other Mexican students with respect; for him it was all about the entire class coming to see him differently. Even Mrs. Tobias commented, "You know, César, you can be President of the United States if you want, you are very charismatic!" He didn't know what the word "charismatic" meant, so he immediately looked it up in the old giant Webster's Dictionary in the front corner of the class and to some extent he agreed with the definition that his classmates found him fascinating following the churning of the butter and that many people commented on how captivating his smile was to others. When he was done reading the definition, he closed the large-scale dictionary and Mrs. Tobias said "César, when you close a book you close a mind!" He never forgot that saying and took it with him well into the future.

    Mrs. Tobias removed the butter very carefully and placed it on a large plate with silver lining like César had never seen before; she then pulled out a box of saltine crackers, spread the butter over the top of one of crackers, added a light sprinkle of salt and carefully placed it in his mouth. When you hear César tell the story you would think that he was being seduced because as a result of this experience, he would add, he came to see Mrs. Tobias in a new way. On the one hand, in Mrs. Tobias he saw a warm trusting person who taught him something that was empowering. César will tell you that Mrs. Tobias had a way of presenting ideas that made him very excited, like those aforementioned. Taking a quote from Socrates about the secret of change and relating it to churning butter, he thought it was a brilliant method for teaching about building and envisioning something new. On the other hand, Mrs. Tobias was the first white person he had ever had meaningful interactions with and this meant a lot to him from a relational perspective. She elicited feelings in him he had never had on a human-to-human level.

César was sensitive to meaningful interactions and his new found feelings for Mrs. Tobias helped him learn.

Like many other people in his life, Mrs. Tobias saw something in young César that went beyond the situation. Situations like this (no matter how insignificant others might perceive them) would overcome César emotionally and tuned him into the importance of a good teacher and ways of learning. For César it wasn't about the butter at all; it was about his relationship with a trusting teacher and support from his classmates.

Later, this became a key characteristic for labor organizing. It's important to note that within César's superlative logic was an outcome (as evidenced by this example) that is at the core of the STEM movement in this country: "...to apply concepts to real-life situations and explain their reasoning."

By his very nature César was a STEM thinker, better yet, STEM philosopher. It was around this time in his life that César came to the realization that no matter how people labelled themselves, the important thing was how they treated each other. His interactions with Mrs. Tobias were all about mutual respect. He was convinced in this way that these were the conditions to maximize teaching and learning.

On March 31st, nearing the end of his eighth grade year of school, Mrs. Tobias wrote on the chalkboard:

> *Deseándote felicidad en este día tan especial!*
> *¡Felicidades en tu día!*

The words meant, "Happy Birthday, it's your day!" It was the first time he had seen words written in Spanish in a classroom setting. He thought to himself:

"A birthday is like hitting the pause button in one's life as a means to momentarily understand the world around you, a revelation of a sort; birthdays are good in this way."

Later in the day he shared his "revelation" with his father and his father had this to say:

"When you were very young, there were a few consecutive years when I would ask you how many stars there were in the sky?, and you would look up: at age 4 you said, 'There are 4 stars,' and at age 5 you said, 'There are 7, no there are 9,' then at age 6 you said 'There are a million, a million trillion, a million trillion billion trillion million...' At that point I realized you had your first revelation of infinity that was also a revelation of your own infinity. I could see it in your face, looking up at the numberless stars, you must have been thinking, 'And all this is mine!'"

His father explained that as humans we develop an immense sense of self with the universe. That's what keeps us always looking up, wondering about life itself, wondering about how many more birthdays we will have and with each year he has witnessed many more infinities in him—this was his love for him.

Even at an early age it was continually pointed out to César that he always seemed to be smiling at something and people like Mrs. Tobias told him that, "He was probably smiling at his own happiness." His father thought that the warm smile he exuded was proof of the joy and happiness no longer describable but impossible to abandon. He thought, "What more could we ask for in a son?"

He told César that while there are things of great interest in your life where you fulfill the goals prescribed by visions of your own making, what goes on in your soul is of ultimate interest to him. He added that no matter how tough life got (like when by the end of the eighth grade they lost their house), he (César) would always have a benevolent presence in his life, most of the time spectral because he was busy serving the United Farm Workers and always away—it's a special tension worked at, loved for, and pulled tighter with each birthday.

So these were some insights into how it is César came to have other ways of knowing different disciplines. Similarly, César would observe that in today's national movement to adopt the academic standards of the widely known "Common Core," he would question whether or not the pedagogy being promoted is simply tedious work as opposed to "churning butter" leading to higher thinking (as described above).

If he were alive today César would also concern himself with cross-cultural analysis by asking about the nature of, say, the third grade math Common Core mathematical exam problems that ask, "There are 23 students in Ms. Smith's class. What is the total number of fingers of all of the students in the class?" When César was in the U.S. Navy, he travelled the world and found many countries that considered the thumb to be counted as a finger as is the case in Germany, Africa and Cuba. The question, therefore, in the "Common Core" is or should be, "How is a young third grade student to address this question as well as others like it, especially in a country of immigrants?"

César was alive during exciting times he helped create, a time when in American society labels for people were being created and conversely people were "trying these labels on for size." A number of examples of collective searches for identity existed. In telling these stories derived from the eighth grade to several hundred people packed into the Baptist Church on the Westside of Delano, César drew an undeniable bond between everyone no matter how they labelled themselves as he knew the more "he churned the butter" the greater likelihood others would see the change in themselves and in society. The white people that joined and/or were in support of the UFW relished the opportunity to volunteer and participate in protest marches. This was not the case in the Chicano Movement, however, as many stone-cold Chicanos had their own internal struggles in and with American society: "Trying to make an honest living in a white man's world!"

Later in life he came to meet other women who exuded the similar interactional attributes as Mrs. Tobias, Doña Dolores Huerta (co-founder of the UFW and spouse to his brother Richard) was one of those women. He observed how effective she was in conveying ideas, in making people feel good about themselves and how people would most often succumb to the contagion of vitality in the saying she made popular:

¡Si se puede! (Yes, we can!)

In her own charismatic way, she moved millions of people to action with this powerful message over several decades, even President Obama borrowing "¡Si se puede!" to "Yes we can!" as a slogan for his candidacy. To be sure, sometimes Dolores acted more Chicana than at other times and César was okay with that, yet they both knew it wasn't about how they labelled themselves, it was all about how they treated each other. It was this characteristic in Mrs. Tobias that gave rise to the concept of Honorary Chicanos and Honorary members of the UFW. He saw Mrs. Tobias as an Honorary Member of both. People believed it was César who came up with the popular slogan, "¡Si se puede!" but in truth it was Huerta so, as the UFW began adding people at such a rapid pace, it simply didn't matter as long as it was effective for the entire organization.

César's younger brother Richard contributed the symbol of the UFW on the image of the black eagle in a backdrop of deep red coloring, yet it was not widely known; it worked and that was important to César. Hence, it was not a symbol as directly related to the Chicano Movement as outsiders might think so, yet it appeared everywhere in symbolic solidarity. And at the onset of any protest marches, it was Richard who made sure La Virgen de Guadalupe (The Virgin [Mary] of Guadalupe) was at the forefront. How could you go wrong with the Mother of Jesus in the front lines of your march? Chicano activists followed suit; it's no wonder Fidel Castro in his admiration of UFW farm workers and Chicano activists did not make a distinction in the movements; for him, they were all unifying heroes no matter his disbelief in unions.

It was widely known that César saw himself as a Chicano and so did many of his top advisors. Take his former lead legal counsel, who while not Latina was one of the most committed "Chicanas" one could ever meet; and her husband (also César's legal counsel), a white Mennonite from back east—he was a stone-cold "Chicano." César was surrounded by people who preferred being identified as Chicano/a. While some may say that César had antipathy toward his own Chicanismo, he did not.

For the most part, the FBI didn't know what to make of César as in their eyes he met all of the characteristics of an "agitator," "radical," "anti-American," and "revolutionary activist," as outlined in their profile. FBI infiltrators were especially directed to watch César, Huerta and Richard, but they came up empty-handed every time, unable to file any charges. In reality, César was the antithesis of Chicano radicals of the time such as Reies Tijerina, Bert Corona, Herman Baca and Rodolfo "Corky" Gonzalez. Thus, he remained, never to make the FBI's Most Wanted List until one day he became the most sought after American in the country predicated on the file that the FBI kept on him due to his "Chicanoness." A White FBI agent sympathizer made copies of César's Top Secret FBI file, but César demonstrated little interest in the things they had to say, because it was what he felt for the UFW Movement and what he grappled with within his own soul that was of ultimate importance to him.

Chapter Three:

Table for Two: Lunch Time with César Chávez and Herbert Marcuse

Photo by Armando Rendón

Herbert Marcuse warned César Chávez:

Unless immigrant Mexican farm workers are transformed, unless they become 'multidimensional,' they will remain conservative in their outlook (ideology) and unknowingly continue to side with the far-Right.

In his public lectures, the eminent Marxist philosopher Herbert Marcuse started pointing to César's ideas, thoughts and to the actions of the United Farm Workers; he did so for the first time at the 1964 German Sociological Association Meetings. The focus of Marcuse's talk was "beyond ideology," a theoretical idea he could ground in César's leadership. Marcuse spoke in his mother language, "Dem Lebendigend Geist" ("To the Living Spirit").

When this was brought to César's attention, it struck a spiritual chord that never left him and got him thinking about how his actions were being observed and analyzed by intellectuals like Marcuse, who essentially were both translating and interpreting his ideas and actions surrounding social change to or in the world of higher education into "academic speak." Highly educated people surrounding César found this deeply complementary and knew it would add to his theatrical effect. As a direct result, César came to an understanding that intellectuals were for the most part much like armchair quarterbacks dreaming up plays but never playing in a football game, rarely grounding their ideas in social action, stuck in ivory towers, and that they viewed him as one who takes social action. But in the absence of theory, César often took the opportunity to drive home this point as he had many times before:

All my life I have been driven by one dream, one goal, one vision: to overthrow a farm labor system that treats farmworkers as if they were not important human beings. That dream was born in my youth and nurtured in my early days of organizing. It has flourished and it has been attacked." (From César's speech given to the Commonwealth Club in San Francisco, 1984, published in Vida Nueva, 2006.)

More to Marcuse's goal, to "drag the gown into the town," he saw as César's task, to "drag the town into the gown [university]." Concomitantly, Marcuse's message to César was an articulation (of his theory of "repressive tolerance") with the message that:

Tolerance toward that which is radically evil now appears as good because it serves the cohesion of the whole on the road to affluence or more affluence.

César linked Marcuse's theory to the plight of farm workers and how farmers marginalized them, saw them as something less than human, in turn allowing for the creation of an atmosphere in American society that systematically promotes and thus tolerates the "moronization" of farm workers, which results in a structure of dependency, more tolerance for low wages, austere living conditions, and no health care–what César called "modern-day slavery." He thought it ironic that people in American society enjoyed their fruits and vegetables, yet they didn't make a connection to the people who toiled in the fields to make the food possible.

In the early 1970s, Herbert Marcuse was recruited to a senior academic post in what was once referred to as the School of Philosophy, the first department formed at the University of California, San Diego (UCSD). At the same time, Marcuse became an associate at the acclaimed Western Behavioral Sciences Institute (WBSI) located down the hill from the university (in La Jolla) where I was also an associate. The institute was started by the famed psychologist Carl Rogers.

Marcuse's university's office door seemed always to be open and was down the passage way from my own overlooking the large plaza, which was often a scene of public student protest; a student lit himself on fire there in protest of the Vietnam War. No sooner had he set up his office then Marcuse proffered the idea of inviting César Chávez to speak at the university and wanted to know if I could talk to the higher-ups about the idea. He felt that due to much of the controversy he was experiencing at the time both on-and-off campus (death threats included) that I (rather than he) might be more effective in proposing the idea.

Carl Rogers knew that no matter how much he wanted to bring César to the university, in the minds of many the "jury" on public opinion was still out as to whether or not César was a radical or extreme leftist. Interesting to note is that even at the height of UFW activities (protesting work conditions), the only thing the FBI had in César's file was that one of the members of the UFW had purchased a controversial book called, *The Anarchist Cookbook,* which had instructions on a variety of things from how to get high on nutmeg to how to wire-tap; the FBI knew it was a UFW member because a signature and address were required to purchase the book. Interesting to note is that at one time Angela Davis, former member of the Black Panther Party and one of Marcuse's star students, was also on the FBI's "Most Wanted" list. Through my contacts with César's son-in-law, who headed up the Braille Institute at UC San Diego, I set up a lunch meeting between Marcuse, César and Carl Rogers. When César arrived with his son-in-law, all I could think of was, "If Helen Copley, owner of the San Diego Union Tribune newspaper (directly across the street with a bird's eye view of our offices), only knew what we were up to, she would have her reporters in our office in a heart-beat." (I noticed that my father, who worked at WBSI, was in awe of César; it was a rare moment for me as I had never witnessed any emotional response from my father about anything.) Rogers led César and Herbert out a side door and down the alley to a point just across the street from La Valencia Hotel and suddenly excused himself.

I thought to myself "nice strategic move." Just like Carl, as he put it, "I caused instant rapport between the two." César's son-in-law and I stayed back acting like bodyguards: he was accustomed to acting as César's and I was used to acting as Marcuse's bodyguard as I regularly walked with him from his home to the university, because the UC San Diego Underground, an organized group of faculty and students from the School of Philosophy who feared for Marcuse's life, wanted him safe. Interesting to note is that the Underground admired César greatly and took a cue from the UFW's organizing newspaper, El Malcriado, to start their underground newsletter to the on-and-off campus communities and called it The San Diego Free Press (1968).

Once inside La Valencia Hotel, we sat at two separate tables overlooking La Jolla Cove. Their presence was certainly turning heads in this lavish setting–people couldn't believe their eyes. As our waiter "Carlos" from Oaxaca, Mexico, offered us some water. I heard César speak to him in Spanish and in turn the waiter spoke in broken English, "I not a-llow-ed speak Spanish...." César looked a bit dismayed but went with it when Marcuse (a trilingual with a heavy German accent) replied, "Well then, let's try speaking English, shall vee?"

The two men sat looking mostly into each other's eyes, almost unaware of the beautiful vistas overlooking the nearby nude beach—they were fascinated with each other. They talked a lot about the transformation of cultures, how we live in interesting and dangerous times and also at a time in a world that requires their assistance and that people all over the globe are watching their actions as charismatic and effective individuals. At one point Marcuse turned to César as if a light went off in his head and said, "César do you know that even scientists are watching you for ideas on how to advance their scientific movements?" Marcuse told César that he wished that he were more like him, acting from real life social protest experience, and in return César exclaimed to Herbert, "I wish I had your imagination." Specific to the idea about inviting César to speak at UC San Diego, Marcuse was powerfully convincing, yet he seemed suddenly to have had a change of heart. He reflected on the time when Playboy Magazine wanted to interview him and his response was that he would only agree if he could appear in their magazine as the centerfold, admittedly, it was a great analogy. Within this context, I overheard César repeat what Marcuse asked him never to forget and that was what the philosopher Victor Hugo points out:

Armando A. Arias

Science says the first word on everything, and the last word on nothing.

Following our wonderful lunch filled with fresh paella (the best in San Diego), we met back at WBSI where Carl Rogers took the opportunity to say that he thought the idea to bring César to speak was fantastic, but then added, "We [WBSI] are afraid the institute, which was funded only by grants in its capacity as a non-profit agency, might lose government grants and contracts due to César's and Marcuse's controversial perspectives." In short after all was said and done, bringing César to speak was deemed simply too great a risk for either the institute or the university. As an outcome of their meeting at the Western Behavioral Sciences Institute, César remained attentive to Marcuse's writings; he sometimes referenced a book Marcuse had written while in residence at WBSI and dedicated to him prior to their departure–it was Marcuse's epic book, *One-Dimensional Man*, written at WBSI.

César said Marcuse "spoke to him" through that book, because much of his understanding about contemporary capitalism and new forms of social repression in American society were gleaned from his thoughts. In later years during meditative states, César said he could literally hear Marcuse's voice speaking to him. Over the years César would ask about Marcuse's activities at UC San Diego. When you take a close look at archival pictures of UFW history housed at the Geisel Library (UC San Diego), you can see a paperback copy of the book in the right hip pocket of César's khaki pants. Some of the most powerful ideas César took away from the book were that of the "great refusal," the power of "negative thought," and the integration of marginalized people (a la farm workers into American society). Fred Ross, a UFW lead organizer, said, "*One Dimensional Man* became a handbook of a sort." It was following his historic encounter with Marcuse that César stepped up his critical examination and abilities for other ways of knowing American society, repeating one of his most widely quoted sayings:

> *Once social change begins, it cannot be reversed. You cannot un-educate the person who has learned to read. You cannot humiliate the person who feels*

pride. You cannot oppress the people who are not afraid anymore.

As this quote became popularized, César began receiving death threats and like Marcuse (who also received death threats), his convictions only became stronger.

César's quotes can be interpreted in simple, yet not too simple ways. Reading this quote without much analysis affords people only a surface level understanding of the meaning of what he says about education. When we look at this quote we see something that captures the essence of his values and beliefs and of his feelings about education. In order to reveal the core meaning of César's quote, I am suggesting another way to demonstrate what he is saying by breaking down each of the phrases and getting at deeper levels of predication. Let's begin with the phrase:

Once social change begins, it cannot be reversed.

César started organizing farm workers in the 1960s when in American society we saw the advent of a number of social movements, like ending the war in Vietnam, ending school segregation in the South, ending discrimination against women and other minorities. People were finding themselves which often meant aligning with a social movement and it was like the social philosopher, Gustav Lebon says, the "mind of the crowd takes over the mind of the individual." It was a widespread collective search for identity. The point is that the times were such that people of all ages were open to social change like never before and that feeling alone in an existential way could not be reversed.

César fully realized that in organizing farm workers he had to promote the idea that literacy was important and in his capacity as a union organizer he felt strongly about people learning to read, but that also people needed to be able to read, understand and take action on new and effective ideas as well, such as joining the United Farm Workers. César always stressed:

You cannot un-educate the person who has learned to read.

    César's point is that knowing how to read has power and learning to read well at deep levels of understanding can never be underestimated and is always a transformative experience once people come to see the world and their human condition in new ways as a result of new ideas. As we have so aptly observed in America's past practice to enslave people, throughout our history those dominant cultures that have oppressed other cultures within our own society have fully realized that by keeping those they are oppressing illiterate, by not allowing them to learn to read is a powerful means for creating a structure of dependency on behalf of the dominant culture. This was certainly the overall historical belief system of large U.S. agribusinesses as shown by their mentality and poor treatment of farm workers. Many people would argue that this is still the case as shown by long-standing methods of what César referred to as "modern day slavery."

    Moreover, at the same time César promoted the idea of literacy, he also promoted the idea of unionizing and for many farm workers from Mexico this posed an ideological problem as labor unions were simply non-nonexistent in Mexico and people continued their allegiance to Mi Patria (My Mother country), so it was at first a difficult path for him to lead people; it was a hard sell. Through his efforts, however, César found that once he educated farm workers about the benefits of unionizing he could not un-educate them–this, of course, was the point. Luis Valdez felt that through the advent of the Teatro Campesino, he and César were increasing literacy, transforming people's values, getting people to see their own human condition in new ways and getting them to join the UFW. For Luis, the transformational process in this way was another way of presenting his personal goal and febrile thought processes for "turning Mexican nationals into Chicanos." This is what both he and César gleaned from Marcuse's epic book, *One Dimensional Man*. So again, Marcuse actually warned César that unless immigrant Mexican farm workers are transformed, unless they become "multidimensional," they will remain conservative in their outlook (ideology) and unknowingly continue to side with the far Right.

Marcuse encouraged César to write up his strategies and experiences as case studies in the form of what he called a "Manual for Organizing and Social Change," but to no avail as César met an untimely death. Such are the vagaries of creativity. Besides, symbolically César treated *One Dimensional Man* very much like such a manual. They both agreed that people everywhere had begun taking notice of the successful outcomes of his organizing efforts as well as the plight of the UFW. Marcuse's point was that American society was ripe for social change, but up until this time lacked tactical and effective means and strategies to do so and that was César's contribution. César Chávez and Herbert Marcuse were at the same time estranged and enhanced by each other's presence.

Armando A. Arias

SECTION 2 - SCIENCE

Chapter Four:

César's Call for STEM to Foster New Ways for Latino Engagement Across All Sciences

Throughout his life, César Chávez grew more and more curious about the life of professional scientists and of the field of science. He was always reading and had something to read in his hip pocket. Even at the time of his death, he had scientific reading materials all about him. César distrusted science as we all should. He observed how it is that scientists developed pesticides and how genetic researchers altered the nutrient values in foods. César had health problems leading to his becoming a vegetarian and so he made careful observations about how foods were also genetically altered in texture and form in order that machines could harvest them–he often referred to the "bouncing tomato." Genetically altered vegetables radically changes how the labor aspect is factored in as well. Changes in food and harvesting kept César thinking about how it was that practicing scientists often stumbled across scientific findings and/or scientific breakthroughs. For him, the bigger picture was that the spirit of capitalism was the driving force behind why so many people were getting sick in American society and around the world.

He was also aware that it is common that once a scientist makes a scientific discovery, it will be either immediately transformed (as was the case in Einstein's Theory of Relativity) and/or used by others in ways that are inconceivable to the scientist that made the discovery in the first place. As a child, César grew up at a time of the development of the atom bomb by "The Manhattan Project," a team of physicists working under the team's leader, Robert Oppenheimer, and it was widely known that Albert Einstein advised the team of the perilous dangers that a small amount of matter could cause a chain reaction greater than the world had ever seen and it was based on his special theory of relativity, that $E=mc^2$ (energy = mass times the speed of light squared). This remained in César's mind for his entire life.

Just a few years earlier, Alfred Nobel (for whom the Nobel Peace Prize is named), well known inventor of dynamite, thought he was designing a "tool for peace," yet the outcome turned out to be a highly destructive substance that became the foundation for bombs. César was fascinated by how contradictory science could be. Years later as an adult, César noted that when the United States went to the moon, scientists had discovered a new substance in Teflon and square tiles covered in this substance were fitted on the nose of the space shuttle to keep it from burning up when it re-entered the earth's atmosphere. These are classic examples of the un-intentions of popular science projects during César's time that stuck in his mind as proof that science isn't always right, so like a responsible citizen, he always held science suspect.

I am left with the indelible impression that many of César's views about higher education, science, the scientific method and such were formed by his social interactions with academics (researchers, hard/soft scientists, etc.) in events like the March to Delano. He really was surrounded by extraordinary and innovative people. I couldn't help thinking how an individual with an eighth grade education experienced the university, yet in observing César's responses an idea came to me so insightful it inspired this work: how it is that when you take a street smart individual with superlative logic you have the backbone of a modern day scientist and when you couple this with a highly trained education you come to an understanding about truth-seeking, that is, seeking for the absolute truth in the same manner César did for his entire life.

Given his personal values and beliefs, César has a humanitarian view of STEM that obliges us to take into account both the positives and negatives of science and technology, not just a blind acceptance that STEM and all its careers and applications might be the best salvation for all of mankind. That view begins with the notion that STEM can also have deleterious effects for many sectors of society, such as farm workers and other voiceless victims, and this was César's main concern.

César spoke to all of us as "the people" and gave those who perform teaching and research in higher education a mandate to help steer STEM in the right direction. Namely, help prepare our students and future experts in working for technologies and applications in science that serve all of us, not just those who promote STEM as an end in itself or as a source for winning one's place in the consumer class or in helping to propel American society into a future where only STEM literate populations will benefit from the material benefits it produces. We must keep César's values in mind when he says:

> *A real education is not about compliance, it's about the people.*

Although young people today may never work in the fields nor toil in austere living and working conditions, they have come to experience the Latino psyche that has evolved in American society, which is the reason I suggest we focus our analysis of the STEM program by first "theorizing" César Chávez and making observations about the program through his paradigm for looking.

Just as César organized farmworkers in the agricultural fields, Latinos need to further organize themselves in STEM fields and begin to provide solutions and out-of-the-box strategies to assist and improve upon the national STEM program's ability to recruit, retain, mentor, and produce more Latino and Latina hard scientists.

In our nation we have a massive effort to increase the numbers of young people in the areas of science, technology, engineering and mathematics, otherwise known as STEM. STEM has an important goal and one our country cannot take lightly. We have seen the creation and rapid expansion of STEM programs in regional areas that can demonstrate programmatic linkages between K-12, higher education, research institutes, business, corporations and more. STEM's overarching goal is the:

...acceleration of scientific and technological innovations that will secure the health and longevity of the economy–and consequently, the American economy." Ross DeVol, Chief Research Officer at the Milken Institute.

In examining the STEM mission statement, César's knee-jerk response would most likely be to turn the mission of the STEM program back on itself and ask, "What is it about the STEM program that could make it more effective, truer to its own intent?"

And what we came up with, you might say, was so "*Chávezarian*," so within the realm of "Chávezarian Theory."

César would begin his observations of the STEM program by standing back, taking a holistic view of American society and observe that the fastest growing population in the United States is the Latino population, yet the number of individuals represented in the STEM fields is dwindling and he would say:

This is a social problem, a major injustice.

The backstory here would be César's call for a reconstruction of Western cultural tradition. Realizing that reconstructing Western society will not be possible in the near future, César's more immediate view would draw on his Chicano perspective, which would have to ask of the STEM program:

If the number of Latinos is skyrocketing, then why don't we see more Latino STEM scientists?

Or he would ask, "How might we increase the chances of Latino mentorship to young scientists?" From César's perspective, he would want us to focus on issues that are presently being glossed over by STEM architects, mentors and participants. César might also suggest that the design behind STEM is actually promoting alienation of Latino scientists by design, a topic I will address later but one that needs serious attention as we need to keep in mind and continuously ask as would César of the STEM leaders:

STEM for whom?

And, César would keep asking with the same courage he faced farm owners who exploited farmworkers. Furthermore, César would argue that we cannot take this question lightly and also break the question down into these parts:

>¿Ciencia para quién?
>¿Tecnología para quién?
>¿Ingeniería para quién?
>¿Matemáticas para quién?

That is,

>Science for whom?
>Technology for whom?
>Engineering for whom?
>Mathematics for whom?

I like César's line of questioning because it goes to the heart of the matter when looking at the STEM program objectively. Hence, while the STEM program has the appearance of truth (a truth leading to the improvement of STEM fields) in a philosophical sense, what we really need to know is, "Who benefits by this massive effort?"

Taking César's perspective on STEM will shed light on where there presently is none. We will then take this insight and ask further, "To what extent might the insight we gained serve Latinos and civil society at large?" What we need is out-of-the-box thinking? And this is not an easy thing to do, but for César, it was his way of viewing social problems and finding solutions to injustices. He would have praise for the STEM movement in this country, yet at the same time see it as a social problem with a solution Latinos didn't know they have, namely to stop taking the STEM ideals for granted, critically examine their goals and organize new ideals in César's words:

> *We attacked injustice not by complaining but by organizing. By addressing this historic problem, we created confidence, pride, and hope in an entire people's hope and ability to create the future.*

From César's speech given in 1984 to the Commonwealth Club of San Francisco.

When we apply a reductionist logic of critical examination to STEM's mission statement and view STEM through César Chávez's eyes by theorizing his ideas, thoughts and values as a means to peel back and discover what is the reality of STEM programs, we will inevitably develop new insights for more inclusionary methods for not just recruiting and retaining Latinos into STEM areas, but to also provoke and stimulate the scientific imaginations of young people in such a manner so as to encourage behavior towards full innovation, which is where STEM programs fall short.

Said differently, while STEM's mission is a good one, it falls short of encouraging ways of actually spurring the scientific imagination towards creativity while utilizing what we might call "new pedagogical ideas and methods" to engage Latinos in science and train their imagination. This is another way of saying that traditional methods for teaching and learning remain in place (and that's a good thing), but new pedagogical approaches are necessary to realize the full potential of Latinos/as who go into careers in STEM fields. At first this may appear to be a sweeping statement but as evidenced by the real-life examples that follow, I will draw upon César Chávez's paradigm for looking and examine STEM fields, while at the same time identify examples of proven pedagogical breakthroughs and ideas that should be adapted by each of the STEM fields in order to fully stimulate the scientific imaginations especially of Latino students.

César Chávez's Paradigm for Looking at STEM Practices

In hopes of providing new intersections for examining the STEM movement in American society, what follows are intriguing accounts of descriptions of practices within each of the STEM fields: science, technology, engineering and mathematics, which enable an increased awareness because we lift the "veil of objectivity" and we critically examine each field as viewed through César Chávez's paradigm for looking as well as that garnered from Latino scientists. The goal is the ability to take complex scientific problems, issues and scientific *informática* and present these in a manner that is easy to grasp, understand and inspire. The outcome would be to have STEM knowledge revisited in such a manner as to further stir the Latino scientific imagination. Speculative as this may be, we will begin by examining the field of *science* as seen through the lens of César Chávez.

Armando A. Arias

"The Lesson or Making Tortillas"
Painting by award-winning native New Mexican artist Victoria de Almeida
Santa Fe, New Mexico. **By permission of the artist.**

Chapter Five:

Ciencia de la Cocina (Kitchen Science) – Demystifying Science and the Scientific Method

By coming to an understanding of César Chávez's logic, vision, epistemic logic and philosophy and by seeing through this intricate combination and theorization of his thoughts, one can come to design new strategies for understanding science, the scientific method as well as the scientific practices found in each of the STEM fields (science, technology, engineering & mathematics). We can refer to the stratagem laid out above as a framework or model as it would have been seen through César's lens. For example, in viewing one's Nanita's kitchen (Grandmother's kitchen) as a scientific laboratory, the idea could very well cause a cognitive shift in terms of how a young person comes to see themselves, significant others, and science.

César's perspective was that whether it be a Cookin' Kitchen toy set made by the Mattel Corporation or one's own home kitchen, one can come to see any number of settings as scientific laboratories.

> *"The Lesson" or "Making Tortillas" by Victoria de Almeida. The idea is to view the kitchen as a scientific laboratory.*

When you are helping your Nanita (grandmother) make tortillas in the kitchen, think of her as a scientist and the cocina (kitchen) as her laboratory. Think about all the pots-and-pans as the tools you find in a scientific lab. And think about all the liquids in the refrigerator and spices on the rack as chemicals, because they are. You can think of her gas stove as one of the most important things in a lab, a Bunsen burner, which burns methane and is used to heat things up and also sterilize tools. Scientists often heat their coffee on it, too. Now notice every little thing your Nanita does in her kitchen-laboratory and that's her methodology–all scientists have a methodology.

When making tortillas, first she heats up the comal (iron skillet) and as she is waiting for it to heat up she simultaneously starts making the masa (dough). She pulls out a bag of corn flour and piles it on top of a cutting board so it looks like a white, powdered mountain and you notice that the flour gets all over your Nanita's hands and apron (the one with jalapeños embroidered all over it). At the same time she mixes in salt and a little manteca (lard) and quiensabeque (who knows what else). And then looking very much like a chemist she pours some water on to the white flour mountain and quickly turns to throw a few specks of water onto the comal to determine if it is ready for the tortillas she is about to roll out: how the water dances on the comal is a clear signal as to whether or not it is just right to make tortillas. And you should know that scientists always use their eyes to measure things. This is the science behind making tortillas and also something similar to what scientists do in their labs.

On the surface this seems like a rather simplistic idea, but psychologically speaking in the development of a child at young stages in their lives, Jean Piaget (known child development psychoanalyst) would argue that:

> *A culturally-based idea once presented in this manner makes a lot of sense to the child and will have long-lasting effects.*

Piaget's postulate makes a lot of sense and is known by many STEM scientists, hence, they understand the cultural inference for teaching and learning; they simply lack the culturally-based process of the experience and therefore do not employ such practices. Said differently, the majority of STEM scientists are not Latino and while they may be good at teaching and engaging students in general, they lack deeper levels of predication (as described above) for teaching and engaging Latino students. On the one hand, White scientists see this as a small point because Latino students are learning and doing well across STEM fields, but on the other hand, while Latino students may be progressing they do not experience true mind expansion, culturally-based learning experiences and further development of their creative imaginations as Latinos: they remain a bit *tapados* (close-minded) in this way. Another way of looking at this is that in Latin American countries, approaches to STEM fields is much more cross-disciplinary and in the U.S. we remain pretty much focused on training in one field at a time. This is why we are perceived as *tapados,* a problem curious to Western science that was identified by the radical empiricist William James years ago when he referred to how the U.S. trains doctoral students as the "Ph.D. octopus too highly specialized."

César loved to hypothesize and often created theories about things; in this case it became the *"tortilla theory,"* as he put it (adding to the methodology description above):

> *Okay now let's take the analogy of the kitchen-laboratory and Nanita's tortilla making a bit further and add to it the idea of a hypothesis and a theory. On one holiday, Nanita and her sisters are preparing around two-hundred handmade tamales at a tamalada (tamale making party). They follow a recipe, a methodology if you will except this time they are having to make a much larger batch of masa (dough) this requires them to have to expand their recipe formula: the formula remains the same, the quantity changes.*

> *Nanita and her sisters are hard at work in their kitchen-laboratory when Nanita has an epiphany. She thinks to herself that someday she would like to collaborate with her sisters and make two hundred tortillas all at once just like they are making tamales, but she holds the thought, thinking that her sisters would never agree; besides, Mexicans never hold tortilladas (tortilla making parties); it's just not part of the cultural practice and most likely stigmatized. "You did what?").*

Insights like this often strike scientists while they are in the midst of doing research on something else. At this point, they must immediately seek refuge in their labs and begin testing their hypothesis. While holding the thought, Nanita develops a hypothesis, that is, she thinks that if she were to add far less manteca (lard, especially the Rex lard that you find in the five pound red and white tin can that you can purchase at your local mercado) to her masa (dough) and add white yogurt instead she could mass produce two-hundred tortillas, freeze them and thaw them out in the future. She knows that others have tried making more than a hundred tortillas at a time but freezing them only means they will not warm up properly on the comal because the lard takes on a new form causing the tortillas to crack and not be blanditas (soft) as with fresh tortillas. She tested this out before just as scientists test out their hypotheses when following the scientific method.

So off to the corner of the kitchen-lab she goes and without much articulation follows the same recipe (methodology) but this time uses very little lard and adds white yogurt. She proceeds to freeze the tortillas only to take them out of the freezer a few hours later after the tamales are cooked. Nanita basically conducts a side experiment as the main experiment (making the tamales) continues (this, too, is a common practice in laboratories). She removes the frozen tortillas from the freezer and is reminded of when she used to live in Denver and would hang the clean 100% cloth baby diapers on the clothes line while it was snowing because when the diapers thawed they came out very soft, and yes, the tortillas, when placed on the hot comal came out blanditas (soft): her hypothesis tested out correctly.

The fact that Nanita pre-tested her hypothesis meant that in effect she followed the scientific method, thus proving that her hypothesis could be replicated and as a result formed a new scientific theory.

Only skilled individuals like Nanita, the scientist, could employ their methods and produce such wonderful outcomes. ¡Que bueno!

We can start children thinking about science at a very early age, even using the popular *Cookin' Kitchen*; fact is, we need to recommend to the Mattel toy making company that in addition to the chemistry sets, they design half-scale science labs, much like the *Cookin' Kitchen*. Professor Erv Boshman of the University of Indiana used to teach a course from his home kitchen on television called, "Kitchen Chemistry" to teach basic science. It's a great idea that gets young people thinking out-of-the-box when it comes to scientific as well as other types of thinking.

César loved to infuse the idea of science into everything and in his personal way drew his analogies to science most often through stories (as above). It was this type of thinking that made his logic superlative as well as relational to Latinos. In other words, the logic behind how he described the sequential steps of both the methodology and theory reflects the scientific method. Experiences, such as the one described above, as simple as it may appear, are common among the reasons Latino scientists give in explaining why they chose a science career (e.g., the oral history project, "How Minority Scientists Became Interested in the Field of Science, conducted by the Society for the Advancement of Chicano and Native Americans in Science.) César made social scientific observations in just the same way. Within the realm of the *"tortilla theory,"* he would add:

Not everyone would think about making tortillas like this, I would because it would make the tortillas healthier. Mexicans wouldn't think about adding

> *white yogurt to their masa (dough) because this would be sacrilegious and they would view themselves as "less Mexican" even if it meant eating tortillas full of carbs and lard. Chicanos could be tricked into eating tortillas with white yogurt by their partners who go to college and learn to make healthy choices, and, they would adapt. But Chicanos, too, like to make fun of each other and would probably have to make tortillas with white yogurt in secret!*

Beyond the *política* (body politic) of whether or not you would add white yogurt and lessen the lard (pig fat) in your tortillas, what César really found curious was that both the tortillas made with and without white yogurt appeared the same; he would say about this and other phenomena that "they have the appearance of truth and yet nobody will admit they changed the recipe." This is how he saw social interactions in everyday life.

Symbolically, he is saying:

> *Our lives are all that really belong to us, so it is how we use our lives that determines what kind of men we are.*

He drew upon this analogy in uncovering scientific practices and procedures. In other words, in his logic it was about living the cultural practices of a group in order to understand them, his point being that "scientists are just another cultural group." It is for reasons like these that he felt it was important to follow scientists around their respective labs in order to capture cultural meanings and to keep a watchful eye out for changes that were inevitable to epistemic practices. This is the genius of César's logic.

Photo by Armando Rendón

A "Chavezarian" Examination of Science

Our task is to view science in general and each of the respective fields of the STEM movement through a critical lens as would César through his paradigm for looking. To begin our examination, let's take into account one of César's paramount core values, that is, "to always focus on the people." Knowing this about César leads us to choose the tool of experimental scientific ethnography as a methodology for gaining insight, leading to new pedagogical approaches for analyzing each of the STEM fields. (See the idea of "experimental ethnography" by Ryan D. Tweney in an article, "Replication and the

Experimental Ethnography of Science" that appeared in the Journal of Cognition and Culture (4.3, 2004).) For example, when we look through César's lens at the STEM fields, we can suggest that Latinos study in groups in a bilingual and bicultural mode. César's paradigm for looking is predicated on a view of the *science-of-science* and in many cases his tool for discovery involves ethnographic science that captures the cultural practices of scientists.

Interesting to note is that in the U.S., the use of ethnography to examine scientific practices is viewed as making a *science out of science* and essentially taboo, attributed to Institutional Research Boards (IRB) that focus on liability issues at the cost of searching for the truth in science. Frankly speaking, this is one of STEM's ideological shortcomings. Yet, a number of highly documented scientific breakthroughs might never have occurred had simultaneous ethnographic scientific observations (in the laboratory) not been allowed. For example, in Jonas Salk's laboratory in La Jolla, California, if it were not for ethnographers they may never have discovered the vaccine for polio. Similarly, scientific ethnographers captured the epistemic logic of physicists in the discovery and rediscovery of the "god particle" at the Hadron Super Collider (CERN) in Southern Switzerland in the same manner scientists would have discovered that yogurt was being added to tortillas in my grandmother's recipe.

After billions of dollars in research and the efforts of thousands of particle physicists, they claimed to have discovered what they were looking for, the "god particle," and yet within moments, they reluctantly announced they had lost it and were in a quandary for several days until they found it again. During the time they were retracing their steps, there were thousands of people (not related to the project) mythologizing about the whereabouts of the "god particle" and began making up stories about how it might cause the formation of a Black Hole, creating a gravitational pull nothing on earth could resist and that would pull all of humanity into another dimension. Mythologizing of this nature would also be the case when it was observed that one could make fresh tortillas, freeze them and reheat them in a soft form.

When you talk to scientific ethnographers (especially those that work in big ticket science projects), they will tell you, "it happens all the time." What is the "it" you might ask? The "it" is the discovery followed by the loss of an outcome (the discovery), that is, until methodological steps can be retraced over-and-over again until full rediscovery of the original discovery. Scientists often make claims about a particular discovery, say *cold fusion* (once an actual claim turned false), because scientists actually thought the discovery occurred in their laboratory, but when they tried to retrace their steps they found themselves coming up with a different outcome, hence, they couldn't reproduce the steps leading to *cold fusion*. This made headlines in the news and it captured César's attention because he was tuned in to the importance of documenting one's steps; again he felt the UFW was not doing so and therefore missing opportunities to convey their good work.

As an analogy to science, you could say there was a temporary opening of what César would call a "Social Black Hole" caused by a social gravitational pull by the successful actions of the United Farm Workers. So, during the height of UFW activities, people from all walks of life just couldn't stay away; the *social pull* (predicated on shared meanings and common values) was so strong that people that possessed strong values and beliefs (aligned with César's) dropped what they were doing in their lives and came to volunteer, in many cases for months at a time. For many it was a rather altruistic thing to do and at the same time very gratifying; it was an era like no other. Today, the *social pull* of the UFW might regain its popularity when looked at through the lens of systems engineering to ascertain the wants and needs of associated stakeholders and how to meet them (this will be discussed further in the Engineering section below.)

César was more than aware of the importance of the need for reproducibility that leads to discovery and rediscovery. For example, he wanted the positive actions for social change taken by the UFW to remain real, documented and reproducible (replicable). He understood how it was that people began to mythologize him and the happenings surrounding the actions taken by the UFW. Clearly, mythologizing their actions was part of the draw, and in that sense helped the UFW recruit. But César was keen on mythology over the truth, especially since he remained rather consternated about how some people treated him like a god because he never saw the UFW movement as being about him, but rather being about the people.

Within the realm of capturing cultural meaning that is inevitable in epistemic practices, "Dr. César Chávez," the scientist, would argue that scientific meaning can in fact allow for cultural analysis. *¿Que no?*

Taste this!

Chapter Six:

A New Examination of Science – Lessons in a New Science

Although not formalized as an academic *field setting*, the spaces for United Farm Worker activities were in fact scientific laboratories for social change. These settings brought together a diversity of creative people (attorneys, city planners, artists, thespians, political leaders, organizers, historians, scientists, professors of all sorts, etc.). It was an activist's stage, so to speak, and a social scientist's laboratory at a time when activists were making new discoveries for positive social change; you might say, "The time was ripe." There didn't seem to be a problem they couldn't solve. These settings caused César Chávez to think about what actions United Farm Worker leaders needed to address and how he should write a manual in order to capture the meaning of their practices and procedures for decision making as well as their sequential step-by-step process for capturing which actions they took to address pressing challenges that made a difference.

Similar to the work of social scientists, if there is one thing hard (natural) scientists live by, it's the *scientific method* (methods model) and the essence of this is systematic observations, data gathering, analysis presentation of findings all through a theoretical framework. There is little evidence, however, that anyone gathered data about the activities of the UFW, hence there were no documented systematic observations made during the height of the UFW activities nor any signs of the application of the scientific method in these settings. As evidenced by the massive UFW archives housed at the Geisel Library at the University of California, San Diego, historians had an abundance of documents but the documents themselves have for the most part been perceived by noted scholars as "historical information," not analyzed systematically nor made replicable for scientific progress towards social change. César used to say, "They [scientists] write everything down in order to remember;" he was all too aware that at the height of UFW activities no one was systematically documenting UFW strategies and methodologies and it ate at his psyche. Even when the documents about organizing people arrived at the library, archivists commented ironically, "The great thing about this collection is that a lot of items have been gathered into one place; now what we have to do is organize them."

It's not necessary to further belabor this point. Simply stated, had there been a different analysis (one more in line with the scientific method) of the UFW's activities, we would today be at a different scientific vantage point, better able to envision more effective pedagogies for teaching and learning, and making different types of contributions to the insight we could add to the STEM such as better serving educationally underserved populations. After all, to some extent this is what science is for. In other words, discoveries are made and documented not only so that others may *replicate* their work but also apply it and make more discoveries adding to the existing scientific knowledge about a field. Even as an untrained scientist, César was more than aware of this, plus he had the innate ability to make these kinds of observations.

During the height of UFW organizing Luis Valdez (movie producer, playwright and founder of the *Teatro Campesino*) was capturing invaluable ethnographic data filming UFW activities and events, constantly saying to people, "If you don't film it, it didn't happen!" In hearing him say this, those he was filming developed a tacit understanding about the importance of his work and in turn he was further encouraged to continue filming both public and private UFW events. Luis was all about *replicability*; this was the idea behind the term he coined, *"tele-dramatic arts."* One would have to dig into UFW lore to locate the memories of loyalty he so aptly captured on film. To this day Luis has a vault full of 36mm footage (archived at the *Teatro Campesino* in San Juan Bautista, Califas) he shot while participating in the UFW activities, and these have not been made public, not even for movies about César; go figure.

One of the perennial issues in the social sciences is whether or not the researcher in UFW-like settings will take on the role of *insider-or-outsider* as this will have a tremendous bearing on the tools, strategies and decisions made in one's own bench work and *scientific methodology*. You can argue that Luis Valdez was filming from the vantage point of an insider, because he was; he had a paradigm for looking at UFW activities so he could capture epistemic closure as he both participated in and fully understood the cultural practices of the UFW, namely César's positive tactics for social change. You might say the genius of Luis Valdez is his deep understanding of the epistemic logic of César's logic of knowledge. In other words, Luis was in the know because he went through a process of knowing; he had knowledge based on real-time, plus he was one of César's closest life-long friends. (Interesting to note is that in my capacity as an *outsider*, I can only speculate an understanding of the epistemic logic of César's logic of knowledge, but again that's what *theorizing César Chávez* is all about.)

From a social scientific perspective had Luis made a pop-art Hollywood movie about César, he would have captured the true realities (soul) of various situations as no other could, not only because he lived them, but also because he had a keen sense for the difference between a Hollywood film, a documentary and ethnographic filming (for data gathering purposes). Again Luis was an *insider* and any Hollywood movie of his making would have been based on real life social interactions, plus he would have incorporated real footage and also based it on Chicano ideology to include César's values and beliefs.

There is an analogy to science, as is the case when scientists reproduce a study or discovery but were not part of the discovery team. When Diego Luna, Mexican-born director of the Hollywood production, *César Chávez: History is Made One Step at a Time*, tried to reproduce a reality he did not live, the movie was a good historical rendering, but an account by Luis Valdez would have promoted present-day awareness and significance of the UFW and how the *lucha* (fight) must go on. To be sure he went through a process of gathering facts to make the movie, but he didn't go through a process of experience and knowing as did Luis; he couldn't feel the process of being aware, which is common to outsider-researchers. So, in absence of direct experience, Diego Luna to a large extent mythologized history, perhaps to heighten the drama. Scientists unknowingly will sometimes do the same thing, because they fall in love with the vision of discoveries made in their respective field and this skews their vision. In Western civilization, however, there is a strong belief that you simply cannot describe science as a myth; in any case, César and Luis saw their labor organizing activities within the realm of social science and sometimes natural sciences despite the methodologies they employed.

In all sciences, STEM areas to be sure, scientists are trained to search for the truth no matter what and César felt the UFW somehow ought to be doing the same; he just didn't know what to call it. To draw an analogy to big ticket science, by the time the team of physicists at the Hadron Super Collider (CERN) first discovered the "God-particle" (Higgs Boson Particle), they had spent nearly $15 billion searching for clues to the origins of the universe, and then lost the particle they were looking for almost immediately. Had it not been for the ethnographers documenting the methods being employed by the particle physicists they might not have found the "God-particle" again as quickly as they did (3 days later). Had César been around to hear this he would have thought, "You see, they (scientists) practiced writing everything down; we [UFW] should have written everything down in a manual!" Taking cogent notes is certainly a key tool for performing ethnographic field research and this is the methodology César was meaning to describe.

In the spirit of research on particle physics, as Nobel Prize winner Leon Lederman said in the title of his book of the same name, *The God Particle: If the Universe Is the Answer, What Is the Question?,* today we have to ask, *If the UFW is the answer, what is the question?"* Comparing the historical development of the Hadron Super Collider and the UFW movement is uncanny to be sure, perhaps even unfathomable. But look at the comparison in this way: take the first round of particle physics research funding where $5 billion came in support of the Waxahachie, Texas, Super Collider, which eventually couldn't sustain the public's further financial support; it spent its allotment early and was defunded by the National Science Foundation less than four years into the project. The reaction of the closure of the collider project in Texas by worldwide particle physicists was to rethink, regroup and reconstitute the project in Southern Switzerland-Northern France. The point is the scientists took what they had learned (in what they wrote down and documented) in partially building the world's first super collider (to the extent that they did) and started an entirely new project in Europe. Scientists had gathered numerous *lessons learned*, but it was also a huge brain drain. As you recall, when the UFW was losing steam in its efforts during the Grape Boycott, César make a trip to London to meet with labor organizers there to mount a protest against grape buyers and it worked; he received global attention. Interesting to note, however, is that this strategy has not been reproduced or replicated since and we have to ask "Why?" My sense is that had César lived on he would have extended his efforts into a worldwide movement and become a leader at the global level; he was charismatic in that way.

Just as many people like the idea of the Large Hadron Super Collider, people also like the idea of promoting UFW awareness. In a world now being staged for millennials who "Think globally and act locally and act globally once again," in order to sustain itself, the UFW will eventually need to take on a new form. From a scientific perspective, in César's passing there was the passing of an era that cannot be reproduced and was not documented in such a manner so as to produce *lessons learned*. Without that base-knowledge it's difficult to build on his successes as well as mistakes, learn, and move forward to make further contributions to existing knowledge on social change–this is what social scientists do in employing the scientific method. In the absence of César's stratagems, methodologies, insights to everyday life and especially for successful social change (that is, a "how-to" manual for social change) we can keep him alive by reproducing him in whatever ways we can. In this case, we can theorize him through analogy as related to his own thinking and that of the widely accepted scientific method.

Just as in scientific communities, the efforts and activities (cultural practices) of the UFW became the foundational road maps for the creation of social networks as a process for knowing about and taking action towards progressive change. In the absence of a charismatic leader, today's social movements have taken the form of symbolic crusades and the millennials are okay with that. Their methods have proven to be effective, positive and have been transmitted culturally as evidenced by recent national social movements utilizing social media, such as "Occupy Wall Street" or "We Are the 99%."

This is by no means the end of such activity. Again, modern day social movements take form even in the absence of a "how-to" manual as César suggested. A problem César may not have seen coming within modern day social movements of millennials, however, is that while technology certainly helps–they rapidly organize (online) and voice their opinion, but the opinions change with the next best deal. Since César's passing, people have encouraged others to "keep up the fight." For millennials this falls on their deaf ears; besides they don't have a traditional perspective on how long a generation really is nor are they causal driven.

In an article in The New York Times by an Op-Ed Columnist Charles M. Blow called, "This is Your Moment," you have to think that perhaps he is right when he says, "equality must be won by each new generation, because it will never be freely granted." (The Opinion Pages, December 10, 2014). To paraphrase Mr. Blow, the analogy to the national STEM movement while expanding the scientific imagination of young minorities is this, "Latinos and Blacks must win our equality by each generation in the fields of science, technology, engineering and mathematics, because it will never be freely granted."

A "Dr. César Chávez" the scientist would employ *scientific ethnography* as a tool for examining the everyday bench work of STEM scientists and come to a working understanding of their processes for knowing as well as cultural practices in their labs and research field settings, especially when it comes to recruiting, serving and encouraging Latino students into the STEM fields. Knowing that much of social life occurs in social interaction, "Dr. Chávez" would suggest we observe their (scientists') interactions with each other and their mentees in order to capture their scientific social reality. In turn, through *scientific ethnography* we should create STEM "cells" (a serious, but creative pun) as interdisciplinary research incubators to study the daily bench work of scientists predicated on lessons learned through ethnographic scientific research from existing STEM project settings. Again, the idea is that when applying scientific ethnography or by observing the social interactions researchers have with their mentees in STEM scientific lab-like settings, there are insights to be gained (scientific cultural practices) that are going untapped in terms of the transfer of knowledge, not only between researchers, but also between researchers and their mentees, (see Gooding's "History in the Laboratory: Can we tell what really went on?" in *The Development of the Laboratory*, 1989). Besides the fact that César only had an eighth grade education, somewhere between his street smarts and innate superlative logic he was able to recognize (much like highly trained scientists) where the knowledge was located, you might say, within the interstitial zones of his social interactions.

The physical scientist Charles Dawkins' notion of *"memes"* (stocks of knowledge that are culturally based) as a society's way of knowing (similar to how genes "remember") is at play here in terms of how cultures both remember and pass on knowledge without writing things down, which is to a large extent what happened in the activities of the UFW during their most active years. But again, this is after all the basis of César's logic of knowledge, epistemic scientific logic as it may be. As evidenced by his understanding of the cultural practices of the UFW, César was all about the social aspect of human interaction as a focus on how to discover and solve social problems–it is precisely this logic I am suggesting we follow to examine the process of knowing and cultural practices of those in STEM communities as a starting point for developing new intersections for processes of knowing and apply the epistemic logic of César's logic of knowledge and for raising the veil of objectivity in the STEM fields of science, technology, engineering and mathematics. Now this would lead to new ways of knowing science.

Chapter Seven:

Science Is a God-Like Monster of Man's Own Making!

César remained suspended existentially over the idea that his life-long efforts to eradicate oppressive behavior may have in fact inspired the "agribusiness technology scientists" to further their exploitive tactics, for example, shifting from the long-handled hoe to the short-handled hoe and/or the creation of new Methyl Bromide ($CH_3 Br$) derivatives. For César, this was horrifying and he remained conflicted in this way until the time of his death. César was not a trained scientist, but he clearly understood the problematic nature of the scientific method and scientific revolutions much like Thomas Kuhn discusses in his epic treatise, *The Structure of Scientific Revolutions*. Kuhn or César once exclaimed, "Science is a god-like monster of man's own making!"

This is all César thought about during the times he fasted. Philosophically, he was caught in a hermeneutic spiral, psychologically the unspeakable truth is that during his fasting he found it difficult to accept the truth about the ugly side of science. When you looked deep into his eyes (when you could feel his humane sensibilities), you could see that this idea was getting the best of him; the existential philosopher Wittgenstein would summarize, "It scared him to death!"

The perils of the scientific method were prevailing in César's mind as shown by the many scientific research studies in his midst at the time of his death–it's all he could think about. This makes you think about his last thoughts. In the face of God did he ask, "Why God, why did you bestow upon us science and all its web of contradictions? How can a god be both just and unjust at the same time?"

In his capacity as the individual selected by over 3,500 climatologists, Gaia theorist James Lovelock reported in 2006 to a group of world-class scientists at the Big Sur Environmental Institute that humanity has created so much toxicity in the environment over time, in turn producing "CFCs" (chloro-floro carbons) that are depleting the ozone layer. He stressed that we (humanity) have "passed the tipping point" for ruining the earth's ozone layer. In addition, he reported that it was the use of Methyl bromide (especially as used in the Salinas Valley) that was one of the major culprits. Lovelock pointed out:

> *One way to think about it [CFC toxicity] is to imagine the toxic residue (compacted dust) of CFCs produced just by humans each year in the past 10 years; if you were to gather it up and place it in one spot, it would be 12 miles long and 1 mile deep; Gaia (Mother earth) simply cannot withstand such toxicity, and so as a direct result, humanity will be eradicated in the next 125 years–Gaia will survive however, she always does.*

This is what Lovelock meant when he said we are "past the tipping point," in short, there is nothing we (humanity) can do now to clean up the earth.

Armando Arias, founder of the Big Sur Environmental Institute, and James Lovelock, Gaia theorist, at the Institute in Big Sur in 2006. Photo by Patricia Arias.

Isn't it ironic that Methyl bromide is primarily used to help grow food and keep humans alive, yet it is also one of the major contributors to the end of humanity as we know it, as theorized by James Lovelock? But César had hope for humanity and didn't want to think that we had "passed the tipping point;" he believed in what President Abraham Lincoln once said.

> *"With public opinion there's nothing I cannot do, and without public opinion there's nothing I can get done."*

So that while César was certainly concerned with Lovelock's scientific facts on the negative impact of CFCs on the depletion of the ozone layer, his more immediate concern was not only to organize farm workers but also to bring to the public's attention the negative impact Methyl bromide is having on the environment and the need for laws restricting public exposure. César always reflected on the future of children in this way, for him, it was not about us, it was about them; he used to say to kids, "Look, look deep into my eyes and tell me, are you in there?" The children always loved it when he did this to them. He believed he could see life itself in the eyes of children and this gave him hope for the future of humanity.

Many saw César as an environmentalist as well as a labor organizer. Being viewed as an "environmentalist" was something he could never get used to as he wanted everyone to know that he was a labor organizer first.

César's Scientific Sensibilities for Saving Humanity

One of the things Cesar found fascinating about human nature was the way people feel so strongly about things they didn't understand. For example, the way farmers were disassociated from farm workers in such a manner so as not to think of them as humans; they were living in parallel social structures: one of farmers and the other of farm workers. It was very much like Albert Camus' notion of the "stranger"–as long as individuals remain distant and/or alienated by design, the longer they will remain "strange" and this was the unspeakable truth about the non-associations between farmers and farm workers. As César saw it, problems inevitably arose needing corroboration and this became the perspective he carried with him in daily life. It was common culture that farmers were raised "not to mix it up with the help," even though the unspeakable truth was that they often bore offspring with the help. Farmers were also reared not to learn names of farm workers, as they expressed it: "It's like giving your pet a name; once you give it a name, it becomes a pet and you don't want to eat it."

Farmers are accustomed to spraying pesticides directly onto farm workers as they toil in the fields; today we know the negative effects pesticides have on the human body, especially the human nervous system and that of any number of animals, including insects that eat valuable crops. Until the 1990s, research had not yet been conducted on this topic. Given the lack of research, César found that farmers themselves really did not see the problems associated with being exposed to pesticides as shown by the fact that they (farmers) were often in the fields supervising farm workers or driving and/or repairing tractors at the same time the spraying of pesticides was being conducted.

Likewise, during that era it was common to see farmers and their family members jogging around their agricultural fields during "dusting" times. Farm workers reported that the farmers had this mentality, that if you couldn't see the pesticides (while they were being sprayed) then there was no harm. You can call it ignorance and/or stupidity, but in the absence of scientific research, that was the belief system for a long period of time among farmers in this country–that's why so many farmers built homes in the middle of their crops.

Conversely, it wasn't until scientific research on the negative impacts of pesticides began to appear, supported by the EPA (Environmental Protection Agency) that awareness was heightened and César began to expose the health hazards humans and all other animals were exposed to. The information began to get at the American psyche and taken to a whole other level.

One of the most dangerous yet most popular of the pesticides applied to agricultural crops sprayed over farm workers while they worked in the fields was Methyl bromide. Although it had been in use for decades, it took years before the EPA identified it as a "cancer causing agent" and it was banned from use at a majority (but not all) farms in the U.S. The reality was that existing stockpiles of Methyl bromide would last for several decades to come and again a significant number of farmers (those backed by backdoor corporate negotiations) had successfully lobbied for continued use beyond EPA rulings.

Ironic as it may appear, unlike the pesticide itself with an invisible quality to it, it was César who made the substance "visible" and stirred the public interest for research to study the impacts on the human nervous system. Dr. David Hayes-Bautista, a professor of health studies at the University of California, Los Angeles, has found that pesticides cause asthma and other breathing ailments that include retardation of lung development in babies, miscarriages (thinning of the uterus walls), skin diseases and much more. César made the self-same findings while conducting hundreds of interviews with farm workers.

In reflecting on what César used to refer to as the "25-year phenomenon" or how long it took the EPA to ban Methyl bromide and other pesticides, he would point out that it took another 25 years to raise the conscience of the general public about its negative effects on the human body as well as the environment. He thinks it would have been more shocking to American society had napalm not taken center stage as the popular chemical of use that first captured the American psyche due to its appalling and wide-spread use during the Vietnam War. César likened Methyl bromide to napalm as its "sister by-product." You might say the people creating these awful chemicals were the first "meth heads" (pun intended).

What captured César's imagination most was thinking about the future of injustices like the use of pesticides, unfair labor practices and harsh living conditions in increments of twenty-five years, César use to say "What's the world going to look like 25 or 50 years from now?" (When César would reflect like this I couldn't imagine a world without him; this is the reason for this writing and theorization of César's thoughts.)

Not long after the popularization of Methyl bromide came the advent of Malathion. César took it to heart and commented, "If it isn't one thing, it is another!" He knew damn well that the nature of scientific discovery was endless and this was a classic case. Malathion took on all the chemical characteristics of Methyl bromide, especially when it came to inhibiting enzymes to interact in the nervous systems of humans and animals alike; in short it was contrived to break down neurologic function in insects even better than Methyl bromide. César saw it for what it was: a chemical permutation (yet another patent) to beat the system while continuing the use of dangerous pesticides–it was all a big political game.

So in essence what we witnessed in American agricultural chemical usages at the time César and United Farm Workers were organizing in the fields was a shift from one harming and dangerous chemical to another and it was all perceived as legal, within the realm of the law, namely the Environmental Protection Agency.

Within the National Institutes of Health (NIH) as well as within the Environmental Protection Agency they also began to take into account the psychological dimension pesticides had on farmers, not farm workers. At the same time the NIH was successfully lobbied to increase funding to study the correlation between exposure to pesticides and suicide rates amongst middle-aged White male findings by such studies. What researchers were really exposing was that farmers who actually committed suicide had for years been reported to die of "heart attacks" or of "natural causes." You might say that suicide was not part of the culture of dying in the farming world as they were perceived as too "salt-of-the-earth."

Farmers live for the most part in rural areas and in small towns and local physicians are often relatives or close friends so the unspeakable truth is that when a farmer committed suicide, everyone including the town coroner looked the other way. When a farmer committed suicide, they were never stigmatized or marginalized; it was simply viewed as part of the culture of dying in very much the same way that even today very religious people are quite joyous even after a loved one commits suicide because now they are in Heaven. As Shakespeare would have put it, "The doer left no sign!"

The ironic thing about the initial research on the harmful effects of pesticides is that the people who are much more affected by direct contact with harmful pesticides, the farm workers, were systematically left out of early studies. Moreover, farmers became the focus of research because the theory was that they were committing suicide at higher rates (rates within their population) due to their exposure to pesticides such as Methyl bromide and later malathion because these two chemical agents were in fact designed to break down and destroy the nervous system in insects; the by-product, however, is that it had the exact harmful impact on humans.

The question remains, "If pesticides do in fact have a negative impact on the human nervous system causing them to commit suicide, why aren't farm workers committing suicide at even higher rates as well, especially since their exposure is 1000 times greater than that of the farmer spraying them?" Scientists of the day found this to be baffling, but César saw the realities of the situation and observing this, he said.

> *Most farm workers are Mexican and Catholic and in their minds it is a mortal sin to kill someone, anyone, including yourself; it is also viewed as taboo and against the law. In addition, La Familia [the family] is far too supportive and important for farm workers to commit suicide. Suicide is not an acceptable way out; you just can't leave your family like that, you just can't; it's against their moral code.*

The short of it was that the National Institutes of Health developed a sudden interest in funding research drawing a correlation between the negative physical impact of pesticides and depression and suicide amongst farmers, most particularly, middle-aged White male farmers. This shift in the public interest is what César found interesting about scientific discovery, namely what it (scientific enterprise) chooses to research and why.

SECTION 3 - TECHNOLOGY

Chapter Eight:

Hoe! Hoe! Hoe! A Shift from the Long-Handled Hoe to the Short-Handled

—Modern Day Slavery and Technological "Innovations" in the Agricultural Fields

Philosophically, César Chávez was not opposed to technology as was Aldous Huxley in his epic book, *Brave New World*, or George Orwell in his classic, *1984*. He was not by any means a Luddite (anti-technologist), rather he was quite an astute observer about the full-range impact that agricultural technology had on the human condition, both physically and mentally. He was not only concerned with how technology had an impact on the day-to-day work of farm workers, but also with the ideological consciousness (macro level of analysis) that is construed as an outcome of research on the systems and techniques constantly being introduced to agricultural applications. One example that melds the micro and macro level of analysis became one of the most controversial and yet most powerful precipitating factors to the success of the United Farm Workers: the shift from the long-handled hoe to the short-handled hoe.

For thousands of years (as shown by human history), the most utilized agricultural tool is the long-handled hoe with a flat metal blade attached at an angle at one end—you might even call it at the same time both primitive and modern as it is the most widely used tool ever. After all these years of effective use of the long-handled hoe even on a worldwide basis, there was never a controversy over its usage until the "spirit of capitalism" (ala Max Weber's idea in *The Protestant Work Ethic and the Spirit of Capitalism*) caused a cognitive shift in the exploitive thinking of farmers in the State of California.

As the United Farmer Workers progressed in organizing farmers and thwarting farmer's exploitive tactics, it wasn't until farmers came up with the idea to shorten the long-handled hoe and make it a short-handled one that César Chávez was struck with how inhumane people can be. He fully realized how a "technological innovation," one so slight could be so effective in furthering slave-like tactics. Even early American slaves were not required to use a short-handled hoe. César saw this hoe as a symbol of oppression. It was not until 1974 that the short-handled hoe was banned in California. Farmers argued that with a short-handled hoe, workers could see the weeds and crop plants better.

By cutting the handle of the long-handled hoe in half, farm workers were forced to bend their bodies much farther towards the ground, causing undue strain on their torsos and backs, all for the purpose of allowing field supervisors better to observe farm workers as they toiled in the fields. Given the arduous working conditions using the long-handled hoe, shifting to the short-handled hoe made field work even more difficult and symbolically by halving the hoe, farmers were sending out a true message about how horrific humans can treat other humans. By all accounts, they were crossing the line, breaking moral rules, reaching to the depths of exploitation and it was a political act on their part against the UFW.

In reality, the way César Chávez saw it was that by introducing and requiring the use of the short-handled hoe, farmers were expanding slavery to take on a new yet more negative form. More than anyone, César recognized the many forms of exploitive practices in agribusiness; he was well aware that slavery was alive and more exploitive in practice than any time during the history of this nation, yes, even more so then when slavery was in full swing. In other words, Americans simply didn't view farm workers as slaves because they had been duped as a society into believing that slavery was abolished, so ideologically, moving to the short-handled hoe was a giant step backwards.

Keep in mind that at the same time the short-handled hoe was introduced, the Chicano Movement was reaching new heights, especially in the American Southwest and Chicano activists were looking over at the exploitive tactics farmers were using and coming up with the same conclusions about new forms of modern day slavery as César. Yet César did not go public with his views towards slavery, but Chicanos did. Not only was it yet another point of contention against the establishment but it was also another example of how Chicanos often reached over to the UFW in solidarity. As much as César was in spiritual solidarity with the Chicano Movement and as much as he saw himself as a Chicano, his resistance to joining forces was simply a difference in strategies in search of solutions. In short, no matter how unfair, immoral, non-Christian, and inhumane the tactics of the farmers were, César saw himself taking a higher ground and aiming towards peaceful solutions.

Moreover the American psyche towards slavery had long been hijacked and we were long ago led to believe that slavery had been abolished. The American activist Angela Davis once pointed out "…the very idea of freedom was most likely constructed by a slave or someone who had experienced un-freedom. Slavery was never really fully abolished." Again, César was fully aware of this perspective and in his heart knew that this topic was well-worth pursuing. He was well aware that, as Angela points out, per capita in this country "there are more African Americans behind bars (in prison) than there were enslaved in times of slavery." He wanted more than anything to make a crossover link to the Chicano Movement (it truly caused César a good deal of consternation) and promote the idea that slavery was not dead, but after a good deal of reflection, he decided that, in keeping with César's vision to appeal to a broad audience, making this point would not serve the UFW movement well. As it turns out, history shows that for his time this was a good strategic decision for the UFW—Americans were not ready as a society to accept the idea that slavery was still around.

On a similar note, the FBI had infiltrated the UFW and were watching César and other UFW members closely. It was widely believed that had César decided to "play the slavery card," the FBI would have gone ahead with their plans to define him as a "terrorist" and as a "threat to this country" and he would have landed on the FBI's Ten Most Wanted List alongside Angela Davis. Now that we can look back, we can understand that the FBI was not really threatened by Angela or César; they were simply in search of stereotypes of their physical stature, giving the FBI "just cause" to stop and harass as many people as they wanted during tumultuous times of protest. At the same time many Chicanos were being watched by the FBI because within the Chicano Movement was the idea of a utopia in a nation-state called "Aztlan," a mythical region covering the American Southwest. FBI agents took this idea literally and defined Chicanos as an "enemy" to this country, wanting to create their own country and "take back Mexico."

César could "feel the future." He warned us of "historical false closures," and urged that we not say "slavery has been abolished;" rather he would ask that we continue with the struggles he faced and continually reintroduced issues to each generation and he defined a generation as every five years. To be sure he remained cautious and skeptical of technological advances.

He knew science had a way of changing situations. He wasn't surprised when University of California, Davis, researchers had gene spliced what he called the "square tomato" with hopes of designing a machine that could pick them and substitute farm workers with automation. So on the one hand, he knew agricultural sciences would in some way impact the day-to-day labor of farm workers. Pondering this reality, a warm smile on his face as he moved his head side-to-side in slow motion, César would say, the "scientists themselves don't even know what they are going to come up with next." He warned us to keep a watchful eye out for unanticipated scientific consequences.

Even with new laws against the use of Methyl bromide, it was such a preferred fumigant that the "agribusiness technology scientists" came up with so many specialized derivatives that in reality new forms of Methyl bromide brought more usage of the chemical to the open market; they even invented a way to recapture the fumes when fumigating Methyl bromide, a practice made evident by the plastic coverings found over such things as strawberries. The "scientific idea" was that by covering the strawberry fields with massive blankets of plastic followed by introducing Methyl bromide gases under the blankets the crops could not only be fumigated but the Methyl bromide gases could be recaptured and utilized over-and-over again. In essence, even though the UFW was successful at seeing through the Federal Insecticide Fungicide, and Rodenticide Act, in reality it caused "agribusiness technology scientists" to become more inventive in order to continue usage of the harmful chemical, thus allowing its use through the 1990s. Thus, new laws forbidding the use of Methyl bromide could not keep up with what seemed like never-ending new derivatives. Even in the year 2015, farmers continued using Methyl bromide from the stockpiles not yet depleted.

Just as César admits, "I didn't see it coming!" with regard to the shift from the long-handled hoe to the short-handled hoe, few people actually saw this one coming, including the inventors of the modern day short-handled hoe as they never saw their work designed to oppress people; they were very much like most scientists, geared only to practice science for the "improvement" of mankind. This phenomenon is commonplace in scientific circles as discussed by Akiko Busch in her book, *The Uncommon Life of Common Objects* —fact is, this is a classic case in point.

Even though farmers said the short-handled hoe would "improve" upon the quality and quantity of work, it certainly did not prove to be the case nor was any scientific data ever produced showing this to be the case. César knew the introduction of the short-handled hoe was a political ploy and/or means for causing a serious rift in the organizing activities of the UFW. He also knew that it was a ploy for oppressing farm workers—they were required to bend further, performing their work in unnatural positions and causing back problems not incurred using the long-handled hoe.

As a tool to oppress farm workers in daily life, the short-handled hoe became the symbol for everything César distrusted about science and technology and the people who used it for oppressive purposes.

While taking into account his perception of science and technology, one has to ask, "What scientific peculiarities might César grapple with if he were alive today?"

Chapter Nine:

How taking a technological suggestion from César Chávez changed my life and that of many others

Photo by Armando Rendón

About two weeks into starting a new position at the Imperial Valley Campus of San Diego State University, I walked over the railroad tracks next to the U.S. Port of Entry — if you had a fairly strong arm you could throw a baseball over the U.S.-Mexico border from my office — to have lunch at El Che Juan Restaurant that served the best paella dish I've had to date. As I was eating this wonderful meal, with yellow rice, fresh oysters, shrimp, pork sausage and more, served from a giant wok-like pan (Argentinian style to be sure, though I did find it odd that I could be eating fresh fish out in the middle of the desert), I noticed a crowd of people forming across the street. It turned out that César Chávez was in town attending a meeting (not a rally) of the United Farm Workers (UFW).

I immediately became torn as my hunger drive and political drive suddenly threw me into a deep and abiding divide. Hey, what can I say? I love César and I love paella, too; the only thing better would be to have paella with César. Okay, César's spirit won out. I packed up my lunch and ran back across the street over the train tracks that often brought the border crossing traffic to a standstill and went into the meeting. As I made my way through the crowd the meeting was winding down and as I looked over at César, who looked very much like he did a decade prior when appearing on the Ed Sullivan Television Show. I recognized his voice as the last thing I heard César say "off-mike," as if under his breath, was: "Wouldn't it be great if only we had a telecommunications signal leading into Mexico?"

And that was it, and then he was gone. Within minutes I found out that César was referencing the telecommunications system set up by the United Farm Workers which spans the states of Oregon, Washington and the entire State of California, ending at the hub in Calexico where I was standing. I was literally leaning against the sizeable microwave tower with gigantic nuts and bolts—it was known as the "ITFS" system which stands for "Interactive Televised Fixed System." These days it would be viewed as old school technology to be sure, but it was state of the art during its day.

I had no idea César's comment about sending a microwave signal south into Mexico would be a "game changer" for my Latino psyche and impact me for the rest of my life. César was not a telecommunications engineer but he was certainly a visionary and his vision wasn't hard to see. He knew the UFW had acquired top of the line microwave equipment and that their ITFS system was powerful; he just didn't know how powerful it really was and that it was in fact already sending a signal into Mexico but no one was picking it up.

Nor did any of us know the programmatic power we would soon discover by offering telecourses in a bilingual mode, bi-nationally over the system. We (non-engineer types) discovered that the microwave signal has a footprint much wider than where the signal is actually directed and it was this technical fact that allowed us to send the signal to two or more institutions of higher education in Mexicali without changing a thing. Maybe César thought of microwave the way Radio Campesina thought about radio wave, going from a low-signal to commercial outlets for raising income? Over the UFW ITFS system César could interact with UFW members across three states; the system also became a way for people to communicate with their families and interacted in the same manner Skype does today over the Internet.

The day after César was in town, the UFW ITFS technician brought me full copies of two successful proposals someone had written on behalf of the UFW: one was a technical proposal to the National Telecommunications Information Administration (NTIA), a division in the U.S. Department of Commerce, requesting millions of dollars to build the massive UFW ITFS system between three states, and the other proposal was to the U.S. Department of Education requesting programmatic funds in order to develop materials to be aired over the system, Together they were a brilliant pair of complementary proposals. The technician stated that when César heard I had inquired about them, he did not hesitate to give me his approval. César was quite keen on "grant getting" so my sense is that he recognized something in my request to review the proposals as I was rapidly becoming a known entity in the community and simply wanted to help.

I also asked if it were possible for the university to utilize the UFW system to offer classes up and down the state. Similarly, I heard that César was excited about the idea of linking the UFW and San Diego State University telecommunication systems (ITFS) as I soon came to propose. I learned that while it would be technically possible to connect the two systems, the federal telecommunications regulations would not allow it. I could feel César's energy coming right through the pages of the two proposals he had held just hours before and his ineffable human spirit came through loud and clear; all I could think about was César saying:

"¡Si se puede!" I began sketching possibilities for new ways to point the existing UFW and university microwave dishes with the idea of making the microwave signal available across the U.S.-Mexico border to the Instituto Tecnológico de Mexicali and the Universidad Autónoma de Baja California, Mexicali. I gleaned all that I could from the technical NTIA proposal. I could hear César's voice in my head, "Si se puede!"

Based on the two proposals forwarded to me by César, I drafted two new proposals. The first proposal had a technical focus and captured César's vision of extending telecommunications abilities into Mexico. I also sketched out a second grant that focused on preparing instructional materials (bilingual classes in science, math, engineering and social sciences). The university foundation director suggested I make a trip to Washington, D.C., and share my new proposals with the foundations he suggested. When I met with representatives for the technical (hardware request) grant at the NTIA (a division of the U.S. Department of Commerce) they recognized César's influence and asked me if I had been in contact with him in this regard. When I told the NTIA representative about hearing César's comment, "Wouldn't it be great if only we had a telecommunications hub leading into Mexico?" he became even more engaged and receptive to the proposals. It was at that point the U.S. Secretary of Quiensabeque said they had been in recent contact with César and that he recommended me most enthusiastically. Hearing this sent me into a hermeneutic spiral as I suddenly felt the power of the situation.

I thought to myself, "Did César really say that?" and "Was this evidence that César reviewed my proposals?" and "Is César sending me a message to do good work?" Or, maybe César thought that if I get well placed in the U.S. Department of Commerce, the UFW would stand a chance at getting more funds to extend their ITFS system into Mexico. At this the U.S. Secretary of Quiensabeque more than inferred that he would be getting back to me after meeting with a certain you know who.

I think that what he was really saying was that César was in town; they would be meeting with him that afternoon over other matters and that he had to discuss my proposals with him. By now things were getting surreal for me. I was simply used to following traditional pathways for acquiring grants and it seemed that all those things I believed in were being by-passed (in favor of the two new proposals) as part of high-level politics and that this was actually business as usual. I moved on to my next meeting just down the street at the Annenberg Foundation for the Corporation for Public Broadcasting (CPB).

I have to admit once again, I was focused on extending the telecommunications capability across the U.S. border into Northern Mexico as César had suggested, but coming from the perspective of higher education. I wanted to do so for purposes of offering telecourses in a bilingual and bi-national mode. I was starting to feel a new project but my vision was not yet clear; in order to garner serious financial support I had to hone in on my intent.

As I walked to the Annenberg Foundation past the Russian Embassy I looked up and saw dozens of microwave dishes and wondered about the process they must have gone through to put the dishes in place and I also wondered about what they sent over their microwaves in the form of meetings and programs. I thought to myself, "Who knows what the Russians are up to; why on earth do they need so much telecommunications infrastructure on top of their building?"

Suddenly out of the crowd of people walking on the street a young man looking very much like a congressional page (messenger) walked up and handed me a note; much to my surprise it was a message from César. It was in reference to the foundation representative I was about to meet, it read: "See Stever. He will help you." I thought for a moment, "How does César know where I am and who is 'Stever?' Did he mean 'Steve' or was this 'Stever' a misspelling?" And, "Was that César's handwriting?" I took a quick look around at dozens of windows in surrounding buildings to see if I could catch a glimpse of César looking at me from a window, but to no avail.

In a town like Washington, D.C., anything was possible. I thought maybe Walter Washington, the former mayor, mentioned my whereabouts to César because we had had coffee that morning; I guess it didn't matter, anyway you cut it, for me life is all about outcomes. The young man proceeded to escort me into the Annenberg CPB building. The bell-tone to the elevator sounded and out stepped a man about my age with a nice smile, a grey suit, a greying beard he kept stroking and on his name tag it read. Stever. He was very gracious and created a soothing atmosphere; it was very pleasant to be in such an inviting atmosphere in such a contentious town. He began by talking about children, his, mine and shifted to talking about how children learn, and then began integrating thoughts about bilingual education and then he said something that caught my naïve self by surprise.

Stever said that he was one-year new to the Annenberg Foundation and that he had been at the U.S. Department of Education when César and the UFW submitted their proposal for programming to be created and aired over the ITFS system once proposed by the UFW to the U.S. Department of Commerce. He added that while the UFW had made an excellent case for funding the microwave infrastructure for which they were subsequently funded, they did not make a good case for programmatic funds, as he put it.

"The UFW didn't ask for anything more than to run meetings over the system and that was not appealing enough to be funded." Stever added that he was on the review committee that turned down the UFW for programmatic funds because it didn't meet the mission of the Annenberg Foundation. Hearing Stever say this I felt something deeper at work here; I just couldn't put my finger on it. He said he was "extremely interested" in my ideas for offering telecourses in a bilingual and bi-national mode and strongly suggested that whatever I do, follow the lead of the UFW and submit complementary grants to the NTIA and the U.S. Department of Education.

It was now very clear that César had been in the very same room I was sitting in (maybe even the same chair) just hours before discussing my programmatic ideas, and that he was helping pave the way, not just in terms of what a U.S. funded telecommunications infrastructure leading into Mexico might do, but more so he instilled in foundation representatives and board members both "What if?" and "What could be?" scenarios for serving educationally underserved populations bilingually and bi-nationally with ITFS technology. Not long after these meetings I began to truly realize that it was not about the technology, it was about the people, very much in the same ways César would always say during the lettuce and grape strikes, "It's not about the lettuce or the grapes, it's about the people." At that moment I came to the realization that the more I get lost in César, the more I find myself.

Within a six-month span and in the wake of a new job, I had garnered several million dollars in support not only for our new ITFS system for the university but also for connectivity into Northern Baja California as César had suggested, all leading to new designs for instructional pedagogy and programmatic plans. To be sure I wouldn't argue that no one ever had the idea of offering telecourses both bilingually and binationally (I just never met them); at least no one had ever acted upon it. I shared my proposals with my colleagues at the Western Behavioral Sciences Institute (WBSI) and we decided to start a consortium of 20 entities on both sides of the U.S.-Mexico border and we called it "BESTNET" (Binational English & Spanish Telecommunications Network).

PROJECT BESTNET
Early 1980's

There is no doubt that César's influence lined up at a time in my life when I was beginning to realize the power of technology and it gave birth to project BESTNET resulting in millions of dollars of support to include massive hardware contributions from the Digital Equipment Corporation for our research, findings and applications discovered at WBSI. At one point we were even contacted by John Sperling, the founder of the University of Phoenix, who offered to buy BESTNET; problem was, we didn't know how to sell it.

So did I take a technological suggestion from César Chávez and create and lead a project that changed the lives of thousands of educationally underserved students in the U.S., Northern Mexico, Europe and Africa, you're damn right I did! It's even become a way of life. At the time I founded project BESTNET, César was there cheering me on (from the wings) and I said to myself, "I will dedicate my life to doing the same for others!"

I took a technological suggestion from César Chávez and it changed the lives of thousands of bilingual learners in a bi-national virtual learning environment. "¡Si se puede!"

Que viva César Chávez!

Chapter Ten:

"Gentler" Forms of Social Control and Domination:

Unmanned Aerial Vehicle (UAV) Drones in the Agricultural Fields

Ranchers today, rather than fly a plane over their fields, are adapting drones for purposes of surveillance. The use of drones in American society is growing in popularity in the form of flying objects the size of a pizza carrying light-weight mini-cameras which can be purchased without a license for an average price of 100$ to $200. Larger-scale drones or what they call Unmanned Aerial Vehicle (UAV) and run an average of 10- to-15 feet in length; the military utilizes UAVs that can weigh several hundred pounds. The mid-sized drone can be navigated from as far as one mile away with a stick-like wireless remote control box.

The Case of the Great Salinas Valley: "The Salad Bowl of the World"

In California, drones are commonplace in the great Salinas Valley, a one-hundred mile stretch of agricultural fields located adjacent to the Santa Lucia Mountains. The Salinas Valley can be spotted from outer-space via satellite as a large green area known as the "salad bowl of the world." The Salinas River runs parallel to much of the region, home to the former Spreckles Sugar Mill where John Steinbeck was once employed as a sugar-beet packer and got ideas for many of his stories. And the old jail house where César Chávez was once shackled during the height of the UFW movement for reasons never made fully apparent is only a few miles away, not far from the UFW Foundation. The agricultural industry is said to bring in well over $8.3 billion per year to the region.

If we were to tour César through the Salinas Valley today he would put together a vision something like this: he would see how it is that the valley has flourished for agribusiness utilizing every square foot to grow vegetables and he would inquire about the human condition of farm workers. César would want to know if Mexican nationals value unionization. He would note the beauty of the valley and the surrounding mountain ranges. He would reflect on the fact that the Annual Salinas Airshow attracts stunt pilots because they have a vast airspace over the agriculture fields. He would wonder to what extent Methyl bromide derivatives were still being used and whether or not farmers are still spraying pesticides (surreptitiously or otherwise) while farm workers toil in the fields and he would ask if the rates of cancer in women and small children had risen over the years. He would want to know to what extent the nutritious value of fruits and vegetables has diminished as a result of gene splicing.

César would be especially curious about the recent discovery (made by the U.S. Geological Agency) of large oil deposits located some two miles below the Salinas Valley and whether or not the people of Monterey County agree to allow corporations to start fracking (a controversial method for inducing high power streams of water to extract oil from between rocks far beneath the surface). He would also examine the impact fracking will have on the agriculture industry, whether or not the reuse of water from fracking has nutritious value and ponder whether the oil (shale) industry will take over agribusiness in the near future.

And he would ask, "What new forms of 'gentler' social control and domination have arisen in the past few years?"

The Salinas Valley is located in Monterey County, home to some of the wealthiest people in the world who choose to live in nearby Pebble Beach and also home to some of the poorest people in the United States, farm workers living in dilapidated housing. Historically, farmers in the agricultural industry in the Salinas Valley played a major role in anti-union and anti-labor organizing activities. About a mile from where Highway 68 leads in from the Monterey Bay directly into the heart of the Salinas Valley and meets River Road is a miniature airport landing field for model airplanes propelled by miniature gas motors.

Five years ago a scientist from nearby Silicon Valley brought a set of drones to the model airplane site and began testing them by flying low over hundreds of acres of agricultural fields. As it turned out it was a perfect site because it had an asphalt landing strip, flag poles, a staging area, fenced-in areas and a parking lot overlooking the great Salinas Valley. It didn't take long for word to get out about the drones and every weekend the parking lot was full of drone research scientists and would-be financial backers; hobbyists, too, from Pebble Beach were showing up to take lessons on how to fly the drones. At one point when the Annual Salinas Rodeo came to town, drone scientists began promoting their use to ranchers and farmers for surveillance purposes. As a direct result, the Silicon Valley scientists started taking orders for dozens of low-flying drones equipped with video cameras.

The Role of Technology and "Gentler" Forms of Social Control and Domination

Using drones to survey farms and ranches is a classic case of what César used to say about the nature of technology: "Even the scientists don't know how their inventions will be utilized. Think about it, it's just a matter of time." For César it was simply a matter of time before people started putting together ideas about how to provide new forms of surveillance for ranchers and farmers; technological change in this way held César's imagination, especially as he observed similarities between geographical space, people, their needs and technology.

Beyond military usages whose strategy is to use unmanned drones to "take out" specific enemies while doing little if any harm to innocent bystanders, drones are utilized in a variety of like situations. In some regions like the Silicon Valley, they are even commonplace as there has not yet been an official ruling against their use. People on the street in nearby Palo Alto and Menlo Park and/or near the Dumbarton Bridge near Facebook often gather to watch them and are amused when the lightweight Bebop drone with its four propellers suspends itself directly overhead as if wanting further interaction and yet the navigator is nowhere in sight. It is at the very least, the least intrusive form of voyeurism at its very best and people welcome it like a new-found toy not knowing who may be lurking behind the swizzle stick. Drones are especially welcomed in beach areas were they patrol the shallow waters for sharks.

Drones were only a thing of science fiction when César was organizing farm workers. He would for certain see them as a "gentler" form of social control and domination and comment like he always did about new usages for technology, "We certainly didn't see that one coming, hijole!"

Today, mid-sized drones are appearing everywhere; they are in fact now part of the American psyche. You find them playing active roles in the plots behind best-selling books like in P.G. Wodehouse's novels, *Drones Club* and *The Culture*. Similarly, the popular television series Star Trek introduced "humanoids" assimilated by the Borg and they were drone-like. It wasn't long after the appearance of humanoids that we saw the appearance of robotic helpers in *Silent Running* and slave citizens in Sid Meier's *Alpha Centauri*: it's no wonder César held in contempt research scientists at the University of California, Davis, who are working so diligently on drone robots ("slave citizens") that could in the near future displace farm workers in the agricultural fields; they are of the drone generation. And, when then Secretary of Defense Leon Panetta ordered the use of an UAV to ascertain the whereabouts of the world's most wanted terrorist, Osama Bid Laden, drones suddenly moved to the center of the American psyche, especially as they were utilized as spy machines and tools for destruction of specified targets–as weapons, they are very accurate.

During César's time, robotics were (and still are) popular and there was a lot of talk about displacement of labor intense jobs being taken over by robots. César kept this in mind because this was at the forefront of research he read about coming out of what he called "aggie schools" like Cal Poly, Colorado State University, Texas A&M University and the University of California at Davis, and so César kept an eye out for new technological developments in the science of agriculture. In line with research on ways to alter agricultural labor were new ideas about how farmers and their field supervisors could supervise and manage farm workers so when farmers decided to shift from the long-handled hoe to the short-handled how César's long-standing beliefs about science were reified, he just never knew what was coming next: how could we? César would always say, "I didn't see it coming!" He would project into the minds of farmers and what he summarized was that for farmers managing farm workers while in the fields was all about surveillance.

On the one hand, using drones for surveillance of agricultural fields as well as to watch and manage farm workers represents the epitome of George Orwell's notion of "Big Brother" as expressed in his book *1984* (1949). Orwell was, you might say, a bit paranoid about being watched by the omnipresent government surveillance; on the other hand, he had excellent points about independent thinking and social injustices. The principle of human observation is today quite pervasive. It was inevitable that farmers would adapt technologies such as drones and new technological designs for agricultural fields to maximize production as tools and of social control. César Chávez was once required to read *1984* and what he learned was that Big Brother (snitches, stoolies and ratfinks) would be watching every move of members of respective labor forces, especially those working in assembly lines or factories and the like, but in agricultural fields? Foucault, while in residence at the University of California, Berkeley, commenting on where technological innovations might take us, made these observations of farm workers as he did with inmates in prison:

> *Since inmates (farmworkers: italics mine) never know whether they are being observed, they must act as if they are always objects of observation. As a result, control is achieved more by the internal monitoring of those controlled than by heavy physical constraints.*

When César first read Foucault's book, *Discipline and Punishment* (1975), it got him thinking about how it is that just at the height of the United Farm Worker's movement farmers had created a form of modern-day slavery, punishing farm workers for joining the UFW by forcing them to shift from a long-handled hoe to the back-breaking short-handled hoe. He saw this shift as a new form of punishment, in Foucault's thinking it was a powerful and highly symbolic form of social control.

Enforcing the use of the short-handled hoe was a demonstration of a "gentler" form of punishment; farmers were basically flexing their muscles on this one while at the same time showing a new strategy or "to punish less, perhaps, but certainly to punish better." Foucault would argue that forcing the use of the short-handled hoe was a much more symbolic move because at the time it appeared to be innocuous (which was far from the truth as it caused major health problems) and was a powerfully convincing message that someone (agribusiness) held power far beyond the situation (even on a global basis) and that those in power could flex their muscle at any time and even join forces with other oppressive institutions.

At the time, farmers argued that shifting from the long-handled hoe to the short-handled hoe allowed for "better supervision," but Foucault would say this is a euphemism for social control, but drones? Foucault's philosophy about control and domination to a large extent was about how through observation of people they can in fact be controlled. Take, for example, some of the nation's highest security prisons are in Atwater (Merced, California) or Soledad State Penitentiary (in the Salinas Valley). Regardless of the placement of doors, floors, walls, and so on, prisoners are always in view by prison guards, even guards quarters upstairs have bulletproof see-through floors, but again, drones?

In this sense, Foucault, much like Orwell, would argue that many times it wasn't all about financial gain with farmers; it was about seeking power and in this case it was power over people and over the labor unions. Foucault states:

> *What generalizes the power to punish, then, is not the universal consciousness of the law in each juridical subject, regular extension, the infinitely minute web of panoptic techniques.*

But drones, really?

From Drones to the Mini-cam to the GoPro—Really?

César was alive during especially interesting times at the dawn of a curious era for new technological tactics for enforcing strict rule-governed behavior. Just as in the minds of many, the shift to the short-handled hoe was a demonstration of a "gentler" form of punishment, and so, too, was the advent of the 24-hour mini-surveillance camera. The "mini-cam" allows for constant surveillance that is far less intrusive than a drone. The idea is to "punish less, perhaps, but certainly to punish better." Foucault would argue that by forcing the use of the short-handled hoe was a much more symbolic move as it appeared to be innocuous, which was far from the truth. And like Foucault, César firmly believed that, "To a great extent, control over people (power) can be achieved merely by observing them," hence, the shift to the short-handled hoe for better observation purposes. Philosophically speaking, you might say that during César's time on earth there arose even newer forms of "gentler" social control and domination in the advent of the "mini cam" or portable small camera with a wide angle and powerful lenses. Mini cameras can be found just about everywhere and in many forms.

The point is that with the advent of drones came the idea of managing farm workers while in the fields in the absence of a supervisor and then the mini-cam came along and farmers thought the same, but now with the advent of the GoPro strap-on wireless camera might this be used in the fields for self-supervision purposes? The technological change would not be a surprise for César but the new gizmo (GoPro) would. César would say, "GoPro, really, hijole!"

From a technological standpoint it is now possible to strap a GoPro mini-camera to oneself or to a pole or moveable wire and provide surveillance to a large-scale area. It was Jeremy Bentham's notion of a perfect security system in the design of a "Panopticon" that inspired a good deal of Foucault's ideas about how in the design of physical space people may be controlled. Most prisons, for example, are designed in such a fashion as to maximize one guard's ability to make observations on a large number of prisoners from anywhere in the prison. Similarly, through research being performed at "ag" schools, researchers are taking into account the idea of the "Panopticon" and rethinking the layout of agricultural fields and finding that perhaps the traditional layout of long rows of plants is not the most efficient manner to grow, maintain and harvest fruits and vegetables. Rather it is being suggested that utilizing a triangular design with triangular fields located next to each other would be the most efficient, a design altogether different than found on every farm in this nation.

Whatever the means of surveillance, an important point that César knew was not taken into account by Foucault in his research on surveillance is that when it comes to Mexican and other Latino farmworkers, the majority of them report to an even higher authority then their bosses, namely God, and in turn live their daily lives as if they are being observed from Heaven, and judged, regardless of any farmer. Perhaps we should send a drone to Heaven, and work out a deal with some angel snitch to let us know what's really going on, que no? Talk about historical revisionism at its best?

SECTION 4 - ENGINEERING

Chapter Eleven:

César's Contribution to Systems Engineering and Enterprise Architecture

In the early 1980s a major jet aircraft corporation in Los Angeles decided to do something about a long-standing problem that exists throughout its industry, predicated on a conflict between the values and beliefs of its workers. Problems large-and-small emanated with the assemblage of 747 passenger jet aircraft largely due to the fact that there were conflicting views on labor issues, because some workers were union and others were non-union workers, all working on the assemblage of the same aircraft. The problem of having union and non-union workers on the same site was something Cesar was all too familiar with, had plenty of experience with and provided charismatic leadership in providing solutions to problems people often didn't know they had.

Basically, when you assemble a 747 passenger jet aircraft there are two million parts that must be assembled and thirty-thousand people involved in the assemblage; interestingly, no two jet aircraft ever turn out the same.

As part of the engineering culture in the aircraft industry, this is the unspeakable truth that adds to communication problems between workers. Again, as curious as it may sound to people outside of the jet aircraft industry, even when they follow the same assembly directions, no two passenger aircraft ever turn out the same as there are always a number of variables (from access to parts and materials to change of personnel) that undergo changes during the course of the assemblage of any single aircraft—this is why systems engineering is so important to build in changes.

Even though Cesar was quite busy with his work with the United Farm Workers, he was presented with these problems by senior project directors at the jet production corporation and they made him a handsome offer to work as a consultant-contractor; as it turned out Cesar turned them down, but did provide this advice, "Take the focus off the assemblage of the jet aircraft and focus on the people as people must come to see themselves in the plane."

What Cesar saw in this project was really no different than what he saw in most any social problem. Just as farmers, farm workers and labor organizers do not see eye-to-eye; they have a different view of the world and it's their values and beliefs shaping their world view as Cesar used to put it, "They [people who disagree] see the same situation, differently," to varying degrees of abstraction, what we call Platonic forms. He suggested to the senior project directors that they must begin resolution of this problem by developing shared meanings that lead to shared visions about the outcome of their project, namely a fully assembled jet. The people working on the fuselage would often blame the people working on the assemblage of the wings for things that were out of their control. He recalls a similar situation in the agricultural fields when farmers gave long hoes to non-union workers and short-hoes to union workers, thus causing a major rift in worker relations. The outcome was the instant creation of a "first-class" (non-union workers on the fuselage) and "second-class" (union workers on the wings) worker phenomenon. No one really knows when or why the class difference originated--it just did and was part of their work culture. The unionized workers were made to feel disenfranchised from the life of the project. For the next two years, senior project directors at the jet corporation sought César's advice without compensation, yet César felt he was learning from their problems and anguish and found himself saying to them:

> *You've got to identify the proper stakeholders, and help them develop shared meanings and come up with a common vision for the future of their work.*

Much like what César found in close-minded farmers, engineers at the aircraft corporation had a paradigm for looking at their craft or how to assemble a 747; they had a vision in their heads and didn't want to let that vision go. So, to a large extent, they themselves were the biggest part of the problem. César was all too familiar with this problem as the farmers he had to confront were very similar; they simply didn't want to change. As one farmer put it, "If it ain't broke, don't fix it!"

César found that farmers (like most people in their chosen professions) were really set in their ways and that they lived their lives much like their ancestors before them and felt a reverence for the land they inherited. For this reason, and viewed as insurmountable, no one had tackled the problem of the clash of cultures, that is, until the fearless César Chávez began looking into it.

Much like assembling a jet aircraft, César recognized that because farmers were so set in their ways they had developed a structure of dependency for farmworkers without truly recognizing the outcomes of their actions; they had developed a culture where it was acceptable to have both first-class and second-class people working side-by-side.

Symbolically speaking, in the culture of jet assemblage over the years, the fuselage people had become first-class employees—they were like the farmers distributing long-hoes, hence, the farmworkers were rewarded with a long-hoe (symbolically speaking) and given better working conditions for not joining the union. As a result, the fuselage people treated the wing assemblage people (the people with the symbolic short-hoe) poorly and Cesar saw this as an injustice, a definite clash of two cultures, just as he did the structure of dependency at work in the farmer-farmworker culture. For example, farmers charged farmer workers for living in dilapidated housing often without running water, clogged toilets and no heat. In their perceived capacity as "second-class," wing assemblage workers literally did not have heat in the winter or air-conditioning in the summer, and it was always blazing hot in aircraft hangers in the Los Angeles basin.

In suggesting that the jet aircraft directors focus on the people, César introduced the idea of "social engineering" as a core value when assembling a jet aircraft. He suggested a re-envisioning of how jets are assembled, focusing more on how workers can collaborate and less on the model of how things are assembled; model designs essentially took out the people and César wanted to put them back into the psyche of engineers. To a large extent, he was suggesting a shift from the technical, thus allowing all stakeholders to realize they are contributing to the assemblage of the aircraft and how their bench work fits into the overall outcome (final product), which would integrate the social. Moreover, what César suggested in his idea of "social engineering" was that in the application of systems engineering and enterprise architecture (showing how every piece of the aircraft fits and who assembled it), all workers would come to re-envisioning the assemblage of the aircraft. Again, César's advice was in many ways revolutionary as he was suggesting that through systems engineering they make the aircraft literally visible to each worker through an active model that allowed for "What if?" scenarios.

You might say César was a natural born systems thinker and humanitarian and this is what allowed for his insight. The jet aircraft directors saw the relevancy of not only linking all aspects of assembling an aircraft, but what they really learned from César was that by demonstrating to each worker and stakeholder their contribution and/or perspective, any model predicated on enterprise architecture of this sort clarified each other's respective contributions to the overall jet assemblage. Because César was not part of the team, he was never credited for his contributions to systems thinking in this way, nor was he ever compensated for his advice.

Systems engineering strategies stemming from jet aircraft assemblage (as above) spread quickly to hundreds of maquiladoras (assembly plants) along the U.S.–Mexico border and enterprise architecture approaches were widely adapted by major jet aircraft corporations, including General Dynamics, Raytheon, Ryan Aeronautical, and the Fairchild Corporation. Even the Jet Propulsion Laboratory adapted systems engineering to research, design and assemble prototype jet and rocket engines.

Cesar's suggestions to the logic and theory behind systems engineering was to always start systems analysis by building in values and beliefs into the design of any project. The idea was that by starting with core values, people working on any project can develop shared meanings and at the same time common beliefs about outcomes and goals of any outcome. The value of Cesar's logic, his paradigm for looking at social interactions in daily life, should not be underestimated. Systems engineers were training people (up until this point) to focus on the system first or how it is that everything is related to everything else rather than starting with a vision that the connectivity between things in a system can at first be driven by worker's values–this was and is a very important cognitive shift behind systems engineering which is now beginning to build momentum. Systems engineering was envisioned to focus on technical problems not social problems. Jet air craft engineers utilized enterprise architecture for designing models that would address, "What if?" scenarios. "What if" the 1 million copper rivets necessary to assemble the jet aircraft were suddenly not available from Zaire because their manufacturing plants were temporarily closed due to civil war? "What if" the aircraft corporation had to search for a replacement for the copper rivets and begin using aluminum rivets acquired from Costa Rica? Enterprise architecture would help all stakeholders see the impact such a change would have on the entire enterprise, the jet aircraft, from the weight of the jet to aerodynamics to the changing costs of materials, training, etc. Designing values and beliefs into computer knowledge models used in enterprise architecture was simply unheard of and was the missing link as it provided a major breakthrough in systems engineering.

The relevancy of approaching a project with "What if?" scenarios is self-evident. Take the agricultural industry, systems thinking would be applicable across the industry allowing for probable "What if?" scenarios from A to Z. Farmers could use enterprise architecture to ascertain the viability of, say, moving to organic farming, expanding acreage or purchasing alternate types of machinery. Value added models would begin with the people involved and more to ensure proper and fair treatment of farm workers. Universities that have agricultural science as a major should require courses in systems engineering in order to capture the realities of the agricultural enterprise with an eye on keeping them humanitarian.

In the summer of 1992 on one of his numerous trips to Northern California, César learned that the U.S. Department of Defense decided to close the world's largest military installation, Fort Ord, located atop the peninsula overlooking the great Salinas Valley (a.k.a. the "salad bowl of the world"). Fort Ord was a city unto itself with nearly 2,000 buildings including 47 churches, a six- story hospital, dental clinic, fire station, gas stations, barracks built during several wars, parade grounds, arts and craft centers, a prison that could hold 1,000 men, an equestrian arena, movie theaters, swimming pools, barracks made of redwood and hundreds of homes.

César became especially curious about this decision because he knew that Fort Ord once held 180,000 recruits at the height of the Vietnam War and this meant that the U.S. Army had water rights, 55 square miles of land and a watershed that spilled into the nearby Monterey Bay. It was also the nation's number one toxic clean-up site for several years in a row. Being the systems thinker that he was, he saw opportunities in the closing of Fort Ord that would have a major impact on the local $8.3 billion agricultural industry while at the same time realizing the importance for stakeholders to achieve shared meanings and visions, common ground, on the transformation of the fort.

At a town hall meeting (held at the UFW hall in Salinas, California) to gather ideas for the reuse of the fort, César made everyone aware of several important issues, particularly water rights and the impact this would have on the agricultural industry. He suggested that in order to work through these issues the new university provide the leadership for the transformation and reuse of the fort and apply enterprise architecture modelling techniques through systems engineering. A team of systems engineers was assembled at the Western Behavioral Sciences Institute (located in La Jolla, California) and as data was gathered, work was performed at COLEF (Colegio de la Frontera Norte) located in Playas de Tijuana.

At one point during the course of designing the model, that is, integrating enterprise architecture into plans for the transformation of the fort, César suggested that the team start including information from the agricultural industry in the Salinas Valley in hopes of querying the model with "What if?" scenarios directly related to UFW interests.

At this point, César had an epiphany: he envisioned reuse of the fort as a new university and exclaimed that systems engineering coupled with social engineering would take the fort, "From swords to plowshares!" In our capacity as university planners, we were so moved by his reflections that I wrote a powerful vision statement predicated on César's core values with the overarching intent to serve educationally underserved populations of the State of California, by design, and that's precisely what the university does today, attracting the children of farm workers right out of the fields and into the classroom.

In 1995 not long after César's untimely death, President Bill Clinton provided a keynote speech on opening ceremonies for the new university and praised César for his insight and vision and added "...that each and every graduate will have a little bit of César Chávez in them for the rest of their lives."

One is left with the indelible impression that César's experiences during the 1980s with the 747 jet aircraft corporation and the manner in which they applied systems engineering gave him a framework for reinforcing his feelings about what he called the "web of life" or how all things are connected. César was not a trained engineer but it goes without saying that he was certainly a social engineer–in this role, it is important to make the linkages between types of engineering (systems, electrical, social, etc.) because the "marriage" between these fields is what is at the essence of César's superlative logic.

César was widely sought after by major corporations to help solve and provide solutions to major labor issues, yet he kept steadfast to his commitment to the United Farm Workers. It wasn't difficult for major corporations to see what contributions César could have made to their respective work settings in terms of labor relations. The 747 jet aircraft corporation and the manner in which they applied the logic of systems engineering through the application of enterprise architecture allowed César to see how 30 thousand people assemble 2 million parts into one passenger jet aircraft in an environment where no two planes ever come out the same, even though they use the self-same manuals for doing so and how this was all part of systematic thinking.

He may not have known it at the time, but this experience had a subliminal psychological impact that rose to consciousness later in his life.

Chapter Twelve:

Reinventing the United Farm Workers through Systems Engineering and Enterprise Architecture

César Chávez would appreciate the relevance of systems engineering, an integrated software design allowing for capturing values and beliefs in the form of enterprise architecture, as a way of designing and building/engineering relevant solutions to both institutional and technological problems such as those experienced by the United Farm Workers (UFW).

In brief, systems engineering takes into account both the family of systems and the system of systems, revealing the interdependencies and relationships involved in complex organizations, such as the United Farm Workers. In systems engineering speak, this would involve understanding the underlying primitives that constitute the composites that formulate the UFW as a complex enterprise and form the basis for engineering solutions. So what is systems engineering and what is its relevance to the UFW?

> *Systems engineering is an interdisciplinary approach and means to enable the realization of successful systems. It focuses on defining customer needs and required functionality early in the development cycle, documenting requirements, then, proceeding with design synthesizing and system validation while considering the complete problem: Operations, Performance, Test, Manufacturing, Cost & Schedule, Training & Support and Disposal. Systems engineering integrates all the disciplines and specialty groups into a team effort forming a structured development process that proceeds from concept to production to operation. Systems engineering considers both the*

> *business and the technical needs of all customers with the goal of providing a quality product that meets the user needs.*
> (Definition of the International Council on Systems Engineering (INCOSE).)

Approaches to systems engineering are diverse and can be applied to complex organizations, projects and collaborative human activities, from designing space craft to reach the "planet" Pluto to landing a space craft on a moving comet to planning and carrying out the assassination of a terrorist in hiding like Bin Laden. Once data associations are made between knowledge, data, software integration, related materials and human behaviors, and more, any phenomenon can be viewed as complex, e.g., including conversations, the manner in which we would study how math professors make mistakes and then attempt to repair them, or how management contracts are interpreted versus how they are applied. In short, the strategy behind systems engineering is to gather organizational insight and this is what Cesar hoped for the UFW especially in terms of sustaining the organization over time.

> *Years ago it was the idea of Viable Systems Models (VSM) developed by Stafford Beer that first acted as an aid to the practical process of diagnosing problems in human organizations, and helping to improve their functioning. Stafford believes that effective organizations should maximize the freedom of their participants, within the practical constraints of the requirement for those organizations to fulfill their purpose. He believes that the science of cybernetics can be used to design organizations which fulfill these objectives. The VSM is intended to act as an aid to the process of diagnosis of organizational problems, and the subsequent process of organizational re-design. The re-designing process should use technology, particularly information technology, to assist in providing organizations with a nervous system*

which supports their aims, without the burden of bureaucracy.
(From Stafford Beer's Viable System Model: An Interpretation by Trevor Hilder © Cavendish Software Ltd. 1995, portions © Stafford Beer 1985.)

Coupled with systems engineering is the fold-out of enterprise architecture:

> *"Is a well-defined practice for conducting enterprise analysis, design, planning, and implementation, using a holistic approach at all times, for the successful development and execution of strategy. Enterprise architecture (EA) applies architecture principles and practices to guide organizations through the business, information, process, and technology changes necessary to execute their strategies. These practices utilize the various aspects of an enterprise to identify, motivate, and achieve these changes."*

(Federation of EA Professional Organizations, Common Perspective on Enterprise Architecture, Architecture and Governance Magazine, Issue 9-4, November 2013 (2013).)

César was already envisioning whole system environments predicated on whole life principles as an integrated view which he saw as paramount. He felt that the best way to optimize any system was to bring relevancy to each respective individual's contribution to a project, thus taking the focus off the product and placing it squarely on the individual and their bench work. For an effective systems approach, especially in today's environment, César would say that it is vital to have all stakeholders at the table for every issue and this becomes a tool for reaching solutions to complex issues. The benefits of integrating systems engineering and architecture are many.

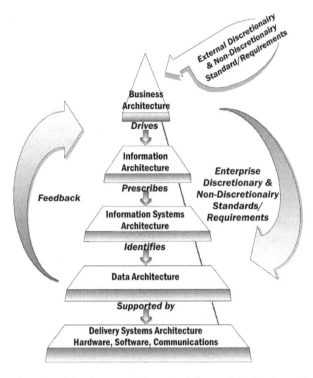

From the Certified Enterprise Architect All-in-One Exam Guide, 1st Edition by Prakash Rao and Ann Reedy and Beryl Bellman (9781260121483)

    Today the idea of applying systems engineering to reinvent the UFW is highly appealing and a crafty corporate engineer would have most likely made the suggestion to César to become a labor consultant in exchange for underwriting an all-out systems engineering effort to reinvent the UFW using enterprise architecture.

    Applying systems engineering or performing enterprise architecture of the UFW would not be easy however. It is not a simple one person task; it takes a team, and for an enterprise as large and complex as the UFW to model all of their business processes in every part of the organization, audit and assess their technologies, applications and both analyze and model all of their data is a fairly complicated project. For enterprises the size of the UFW, usually several teams working on different architectural segments would be involved. This would involve business architects, data architects, application architects, etc., working together in concert with and as part of an architectural program. The value of the enterprise architecture would be great, but there would need to be a strong commitment from the highest levels of management at the UFW and a willingness to dedicate the needed resources for such an endeavor. This should be an attractive and fundable idea to major foundations like the Ford Foundation (see below).

The idea is to orient Latino students in the art and science of creating effective systems and at the same time spur their interests towards STEM fields. This is only possible when traditional approaches break from routine pedagogical practices and transform the way STEM fields are taught. Systems engineering will most likely reveal that professionals serving as mentors in all of the STEM fields need to recognize that when mentoring Latino students it is not just about their being bilingual or bicultural, it's about how teaching and learning attract and sustain their attention in new ways of knowing respective subject matter.

In American society we must come to the realization that continued revamping of our educational systems doesn't always necessarily equate to improved teaching and learning. The Common Core Movement in our country today is but another example of a huge effort of this nature that remains unproven, even prominent politicians that once supported the idea of Common Core are flip-flopping on further support within their respective states. Modern day perspectives on education ought to focus on keeping what is currently in place in education but perhaps adding a new dimension like systems engineering as a pedagogical tool and skill that is sorely needed in a digital age.

University students must learn to ready themselves with applicable skills and not blame their universities for an ill-education. Students who major in the social and behavioral sciences can become quite employable by minoring in systems engineering, enterprise architecture, geographic information sciences and the like; industry sees these "marriages" as completely compatible. Silicon Valley CEOs are screaming for social science majors to "learn how to speak engineering" because the perennial problem in their industry is that "engineers make the worst supervisors over other engineers," yet universities do not train or educate social science majors in this way. (You may find it interesting to note that the reverse is not true, however: you can't take an engineer and have them take social science courses and expect they will become better supervisors of other engineers, it doesn't work that way; you cannot "re-engineer" engineers: (pun intended.) The point is if a Latino student majoring in social science wants to be gainfully employed in "smart industries," they need to move beyond traditional education and help themselves by also earning a certificate from perhaps a vocational school or enterprise architecture certification institute (i.e., FEAC) or any entity that will provide them with the skill that is in this case learning how to "speak engineering." The inference is to add systems engineering to the skill set of engineers in the STEM fields.

The world of philanthropy was very different in the 1960s, 70s and 80s as there were far fewer entities making requests to potential funders for their cause. Concomitantly, since the 1990s there has been an explosion of new agencies and non-profits with legitimate causes from improving health conditions, AIDS research, making higher education more accessible, environmental sustainability, social ecological issues and much more. In response to the outgrowth of this highly competitive environment, to this end the United Farmer Workers created the UFW Foundation in an attempt to leverage both internal and external resources to fund their activities. Even so the question remains, "How does the UFW continue to find the funding it needs to make the most of their proposals?" The answer would be revealed in a systems engineering study to be sure.

Systems thinkers need to explore the corporate role in the future of UFW development and they could begin with an outlook towards corporate responsibility and ask: How does a corporation engage with the UFW on a grassroots level? What are the opportunities in such a strategic partnership? What is the role of corporate social responsibility? What would be the pitfalls and risks? How can systems engineering and enterprise architecture help to improve upon labor relations, education, health, living conditions, and agricultural productivity, and the importance of human capital, open communication and shared expectations. It should not be assumed that the UFW would partner with corporations in the agricultural industry as that would be limiting.

César would want to promote systems engineering/enterprise architecture as a viable tool dedicated to promoting sustainable and accessible technology-based solutions to problems underserved areas don't realize they have and for addressing STEM issues as key to development of solutions to humanitarian problems on a global basis and he would see a role for the UFW to provide leadership in this way on the global stage.

> *Our ambitions must be broad enough to include the aspirations and needs of others, for their sakes and for our own.* – César Chávez

In this light the UFW could become, in part, an organization that enables collaboration, knowledge sharing and skill development across any number of disciplines while promoting humanitarianism. César would want and create partnerships with similar societies on a global basis while at the same time ensuring the development and deployment of essential technologies that focus on emerging markets, social innovation and sustainable designs. The experiences and lessons learned from the UFW project along with its human rights initiatives once realized could be deployed to other countries with similar agricultural markets as related to changing technology and especially renewable energy sectors.

Benefits of Enterprise Architecture for the United Farm Workers

The benefits of enterprise architecture to the United Farm Workers could be achieved through its direct and indirect contributions to organizational goals. It has been found that the most notable benefits of enterprise architecture can be observed in the following areas:

- Organizational design: Enterprise architecture provides support in the areas related to design and re-design of the organizational structures during mergers, acquisitions or during general organizational change.
- Organizational processes and process standards: Enterprise architecture helps enforce discipline and standardization of business processes, and enables process consolidation, reuse and integration.
- Project portfolio management: Enterprise architecture supports investment decision-making and work prioritization.
- Project management: Enterprise architecture enhances the collaboration and communication between project stakeholders. Enterprise architecture contributes to efficient project scoping, and to definition of more complete and consistent project deliverables.
- Requirements Engineering: Enterprise architecture increases the speed of requirement elicitation and the accuracy of requirement definitions, through publishing of the enterprise architecture documentation.
- System development: Enterprise architecture contributes to optimal system designs and efficient resource allocation during system development and testing.
- IT management and decision making: Enterprise architecture is found to help enforce discipline and standardization of IT planning activities and to contribute to reduction in time for technology-related decision making.
- IT value: Enterprise architecture helps reduce the systems implementation and operational costs, and minimize replication of IT infrastructure services across business units.

(The Contribution of Enterprise Architecture to the Achievement of Organizational Goals: Establishing the Enterprise Architecture Benefits Framework, Technical Report, Department of Information and Computing Sciences, Utrecht University, Utrecht, The Netherlands, (2010 online).)

It's certainly a worthy cause to bring systems engineering and enterprise architecture to the UFW environment. With ample financial support to integrate systems engineering throughout the UFW enterprise, the UFW could create a cell for the integration of systems engineering/enterprise architecture into its overall operation that will not only improve upon the organization but could very well become a global solution for farmworkers everywhere. In turn this could become a powerful UFW product if they so choose.

Along the same lines of thought, Business schools have discovered the virtues of interdisciplinary studies and through enterprise architecture so, too, could fields found in STEM. Thus, they are trained in multiple specialties that have business applications and are essential to good management, entrepreneurial vision, and decision making in corporate America. The analogy to advancing the UFW as an organization is similar to that in "B-schools." Who would have thought that business schools would be forced by advances in all STEM fields: sciences, technology, engineering, and mathematics, to go beyond the strict code of game theory, finance, and case study approaches about growing businesses for future managers?

Since the 1980s, the UFW has experienced dramatic decreases in its membership. Unless the advantages of adapting such opportunities in the agricultural industry as enterprise architecture/systems engineering is realized in the UFW, it will pass away as yet another missed opportunity. It will not be long before systems engineering skills will be required in every industry and the UFW is no exception. This is why we need to factor new ways of knowing, digitally and through innovation and entrepreneurship into a paradigm of STEM training for Latinos, which is the overarching premise of this work.

César Chávez would strongly support the development of STEM fields as discussed in this work especially in terms of utilizing human rights initiatives as a backdrop for "marrying" systems engineering to enterprise architecture (EA) and to what he called, "social engineering," as significant to managing technological, political and social issues as well as to providing unique leadership to the UFW as:

Systems engineering ensures that all likely aspects of a project or system are considered, and integrated into a whole." (Wikipedia 2014.)

When it comes to ideas surrounding the "marriage" of systems engineering to social engineering, as César saw it, especially for human rights initiatives, the potential sources (e.g., Ford Foundation, Facebook, etc.) of funding would need to show a proclivity to support ideals backed by humanitarian ideas. As millennials come into their own in American society, we are going to see growing trends in support of organizations such as the UFW but with innovative humanitarian initiatives in hand. A systematic road map is needed to further seek external funding from private foundations/trusts and government agencies in the U.S. and abroad.

SECTION 5 - MATHEMATICS

Chapter Thirteen:

César Chávez's Political Insights into Teaching and Learning Mathematics in Socialistic and Democratic Societies

In 1835, the social philosopher, political scientist and architect Alexis de Tocqueville visited the United States and made numerous observations about how Americans work together. "They are a nation of joiners," he exclaimed. He also observed how university professors of the time integrated ideas about the scientific method and engineering designs in teaching mathematics, which in effect promoted the idea of collaborative problem-solving, which, of course, is at the core of César Chávez's thinking. Interestingly, during the 1960s and 70s during César's work as a union organizer, American society was ripe for social change as people were willingly joining and volunteering for new social organizations such as the Peace Corps and AmeriCorps. Unlike today, the spirit to join was at its peak during that era and contributed to the increase in the number of farm workers joining the United Farm Workers union.

In his epic book, *Democracy in America*, de Tocqueville encouraged American scientists to keep teaching in cross-disciplinary and interdisciplinary ways; his insight was timely and uncanny as his prediction was similar to that of the radical empiricist William James (*Radical Empiricism*) who observed that American-trained Ph.D.'s were rapidly becoming too close-minded about their respective areas of specialization, particularly in the field of mathematics. de Tocqueville took this to mean that due to the "idea of democracy," American Ph.D.'s were becoming "over democratized in their thinking," in turn allowing for the development of a culture encouraging them to follow their research in whatever interests they wanted regardless of the needs of American society. Thus, U.S. research professors developed a self-justifying rationale for actually encouraging the "over democratization" of one's own ideas in a democratic society in the spirit of searching for the truth.

The idea of searching for the truth remained problematic for César because he remained curious about the bench work of scientists, and was always thinking about how science might improve upon the working conditions of farm workers on the one hand and on the other hand keep exploring how this might be possible. During the time of his activism, César found it baffling that scientists did not inherently focus their research on the social good such as researching the impact of pesticides or other agricultural by-products on farm workers toiling in the fields.

In Western Civilization, it was the philosopher Plato who was responsible for having successfully promoted the idea of "free thinking" and "searching for the truth" in a democratic society by introducing the concept of *tenure* in the Academy he created, one of the earliest forms of a university. He envisioned a high level philosopher of mathematics being able to pursue his own intellectual interest without fear of persecution, harassment or death, as experienced by his teacher, Socrates. César found this to be an attractive idea and one he thought might be integrated into the unionized environment. And while it did not take the form of tenure, it surely took on the form of seniority in unions across America, what César saw as a form of tenure. In Plato's *Republic*, collaboration was the tune of the day and mathematicians like Aristotle performed their research in a culture of collaboration. Think about it this way: in a democratic society you might assume a culture of collaboration, but in a democratic society that is also capitalistic by design, an individualistic ideology arises as a stronger form–this is where we are today.

Over the past one hundred years, American society has experienced a cultural shift based on an ideology of *"every man for himself"* and this is highly individualistic. Karl Mannheim (*Ideology and Utopia,* 1937) would argue that this has had a direct impact on how we teach and how we learn in our society, César would argue that we simply "don't share and/or collaborate like we used to." We have in effect shifted from a "nation of joiners" to a nation of highly individualistic people not willing to share for fear of losing something we don't have; we don't see the value of the group or of collaboration. From a pedagogical standpoint, this has been the downfall of STEM fields in American society. Millennials give off the illusion that they are joiners as they will vote for something that is momentarily appealing, but change their vote just as fast when presented with a better deal. César remained consternated over this problem and dedicated his life to the idea of furthering a culture of collaboration.

> *César Chávez is all about cultivating a culture of collaboration and sees it within every aspect of society from social movements (social change) to scientific thought to teaching and learning mathematics.* –Sonny Boy Arias

As distant as the ideas of teaching, learning and ideology might seem, Mannheim (1937) makes an uncanny yet spot-on connection. This point cannot be taken lightly as even as far back as the early 1800s, both James and de Tocqueville were sensing that while democracy can be a good thing for American society, it can also have its downfalls in terms of how it encourages Ph.D.-trained researchers to follow a special research interest with no end in sight; this problem is pervasive in the fields represented in the present-day STEM movement for improving our citizenry to fully participate in the fields of science, technology, engineering and mathematics. The exception, STEM mentors in the field of mathematics, are seemingly more collaborative as shown by the high number of authors often placed on publications in professional mathematical journals–they must really believe in the power of numbers [pun intended].

Moreover, at a macro level of analysis the idea that democratic thinking affects scientific inquiry is certainly not new in terms of such matters as the politics of funding and the types of research that is funded. What James and de Tocqueville were sensing, however, is much deeper than politics; what they were observing at the bench work level of scientific inquiry was what and how a scientific researcher is to determine what they will spend their time researching. In his book, *Science in a Free Society*, Paul Feyerabend grapples with this notion inasmuch as he says, "that while scientists are encouraged to follow their respective interests regardless of overall societal needs," yet for the past several decades the National Science Foundation (NSF) has provided the majority of its funding in each of the respective STEM areas. In a democratic society, this is all fine and many would argue that the NSF is indeed meeting its mission.

Conversely, in the early 1800s the American scientific intellect experienced a radical departure from collaborative approaches to individualistic approaches to scientific inquiry, what William James came to refer to as the "Ph.D. octopus," a metaphor for how researchers are trained in only one paradigm for looking at their discipline, somehow connect to a larger body of knowledge, but without knowing the linkages to other fields. In this regard one has to ask: What does the field of mathematics look like from other political perspectives? It is a worthy question and one that captured César's imagination.

Math Large

What we find in American society today are curious movements dealing with experimental pedagogical approaches to teaching math and to changing physical structures where teaching is done. In order to accommodate these experiments, César would observe that these movements are due to the evolution of what came out of the 1960s and from the UFW's recruitment efforts, he once said "people are tired of collaboration and simply want to see if they can figure out life on their own." So what we find today is an even more curious attempt at trying to solve the problem of how to successfully teach math in an atmosphere of budget cutbacks and growing numbers of students, especially Latino students.

A few years ago a major university in Southern California boasted about the fact that they had converted their old gymnasium into a classroom that held in excess of 600 students. The front page of the local paper showed a picture with a professor standing beneath a basketball hoop and scoreboard with a sea of students in the background. Was it my imagination or did the scoreboard read: "Students 600, Professor 1?" Another university in California followed suit and coined the term *"Math Large"* that caught on throughout the state as the "preferred" method for teaching math. One just has to ask: "Is bigger better?" and "Is this the spirit of the STEM movement in our country?" As a strong-minded union organizer looking out for the interest of the people, César's knee-jerk response to Math Large would have been an examination of labor exploitation issues in student-professor ratios, 600 students to 1 professor. Talk about power in numbers.

In Northern California, a university bought into the "Moog-movement," or adding math courses available to the entire world with "thousands-upon-thousands" of students participating in online courses. The efficacy of such an approach is dizzying, ¿que no? Learning math online is somewhere between taking an online chemistry class or practicum in nursing; there is nothing like hands-on teaching. The drop-out rates are extremely high in these settings; they're more of a method for turning students off to math.

Some online math classes however do provide good content-knowledge for the self-learner that would complement Math Large, e.g., Coursera, which provides some evidence that in an age of individualistically minded millennials self-paced learning is possible, but only with excellent materials. Just don't recommend a brain surgeon who earned his medical degree, online. Conversely, there is also a movement in our country towards collaborative approaches to teaching and learning mathematics based on cross-disciplinary and interdisciplinary research and teaching– this is certainly the overarching idea at CREATE (Center for Research on Educational Equity,

Assessment and Teaching Excellence) located at the University of California, San Diego. Now that the embargo is being lifted in Cuba we find a national shift back to collaborative learning and researching in this country. César believed in collaborative everything and was street smart; he knew intuitively that within a group of people social problems as well as math problems could be solved. This intuition was taken to a new level, however, as he organized meetings, rallies and marches so that no matter what problem arose, there was always a diversity of people supporting the UFW, professional engineers, scientists, mathematicians, attorneys, physicians, school teachers, laborers. He got the feeling that there wasn't a problem they couldn't solve, and he took this feeling with him everywhere he went; some problems took longer to solve than others, but that, too, became a factor in approaching problem solving. He saw teaching and learning math in the same way.

This is the essence in *theorizing* César Chávez values and beliefs when searching for solutions to learning math. In other words, just as we find in social problems that it is important to uncover the truth and in so doing often ascertain pedagogical problems, math professors (teachers of math at every level) do not fully realize their situation and/or that they are in fact part of what César calls the "social calculus."

There are perennial issues within the realm of teaching and learning math. For instance, those who teach math know that just because a student may pass a math class doesn't necessarily mean he understands the subject matter. There are students who love math, but do not do well, get below average grades, and continue onto higher levels of math. For most professors and students "Math Large" simply doesn't work, it's too big and the drop-out rate is always high and frankly students in these types of situations develop a distain for math, never to return. If it were not driven by budget cuts, no one would be experimenting with large-scale efforts to teach math.

So in a "Chavezarian" examination of mathematics, we are not talking about the actual mathematics, *per se*; we are focused rather on the *social* which includes everything from labor issues related to teacher's workload to the actual teaching and learning of math, hence, César's idea of "social calculus" which is a stronger form than only math because it also integrates math. Similarly, César would find it rather curious that the idea of "Math Large" was conceived and be driven to make direct observations to see how it "gets done." How then does one teach math to 600 students all at the same time and why would one want to do so? In a case such as this, his focus would not be on any particular ethnic group, but rather on anyone being exploited. César would want to know the "Why?"

In the world of agricultural sciences, genetic engineers are constantly experimenting with altering vegetables in order that they may be harvested by machines, the outcome being similar to Math Large: you win some and you lose some. You may be able to genetically alter the physical make-up of a tomato so that the outer skin is pliable enough for a machine to harvest and replace thousands of individuals, but you lose the nutritional value.

Moreover, in theorizing César Chávez and at the same time becoming Latino specific, he assists our thinking and asks the question, "How it is that Latinos can learn math more thoroughly in innovative instructional settings (like Math Large) and at the same time develop a *mathematical imagination* and become inspired by the experience?" How do you spell "Hi-jo-le?

The STEM program encourages Latinos to study math at higher levels than most, but it does not address the issue of how Latinos learn and/or how Latinos upon learning math might improve their grades, their learning skills, social behavior and in turn inspire research that would result in innovative and creative teaching methods, as in situations such as "Math Large," online and/or learning from teachers and professors who lack experience in serving educationally underserved populations–that would be César's point.

Keep in mind César's idea that, "It's not about the math, it's about the people." This would be his mindset. If he were alive today he would likely make the following suggestions when serving Latinos:

- Identify Spanish-speaking professors from the U.S or from other countries who obtained a Ph.D. in Mathematics from reputable U.S. institutions.
- Utilize a known Calculus One book that is available in both English and Spanish.
- Have the professor first teach a chapter in English, take a break and form a discussion group (speaking in English) and have students describe in their own words how to solve the math problem.
- Now have the same professor teach the self-same chapter in Spanish, take a break and form a discussion group (speaking only in Spanish) and have students describe in their own words how to solve the math problem.
- To further expand on instructional online pedagogy, employ an online video-conferencing ability while following the steps above, but now adding students from online classes located in Mexico and/or Cuba and in the U.S., allowing for groups of students to meet and grapple with math problems first in English and then in Spanish.
- In addition most learning software, such as iLearn, Angel and Blackboard will all complement the creation of a bilingual online learning atmosphere.

This is the type of scientific research César would have loved to see and experience. He would have loved to see students in learning settings as described above with outcomes such as these:

- Studying math in this mode, students would learn math more thoroughly.
- They would improve their language competency in Spanish and/or English.
- Students would come to see their native language as an asset.
- Students would find that classes taught in this manner often also act as elocution lessons to temper one's accent in both languages.
- They will actively seek higher levels of mathematics.

- As a result of the findings above they experience higher levels of interest in STEM (science, technology, engineering and mathematics) fields of study.
- Students will also experience higher levels of self-esteem.

Whether it be in the agricultural fields or in the STEM fields, César simply wants everyone to succeed.

Chapter Fourteen:

The Mathematical Imagination and Social Calculus of César Chávez

Math is not just solving for X; it is also for figuring out why?"
—Arthur Benjamin, professor of mathematics at Harvey Mudd College.

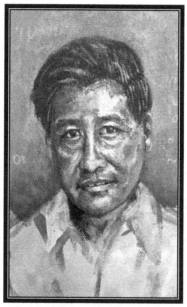

From painting by Gabriella Borges

In theorizing César Chávez, let's ask, "How did César know math?" not in terms of actual mathematical formulas and equations, but the general meaning and logic of math and its applications and how it is experienced in daily life. How did he experience it? What did he have to say about it? With or without a Ph.D. in mathematics, César Chávez viewed mathematics as a thought process for explaining how things change in the world;

he would say, "Calculus explains a form of social change and social change is all about calculus." People around him, not knowing what he meant and/or what he might say next, would be set back by his comments.

César is a solutions strategist to be sure and was perceived as such by others who would often devise strategies for thinking out-of-the-box. As shown by the examples provided above, he found solutions to problems people in STEM fields didn't know they had, particularly when serving Latinos. Given his values and beliefs and how he looked out at the world, what follows are observations César would have made and are quite revealing; they shed new light on a perennial problem or that of teaching and learning mathematics, hence, the social calculus of César Chávez.

César was not a highly trained mathematician but he loved numbers and found and applied a curious logic behind them; it wasn't so much about the math as it was the logic of using, applying and presenting numbers that captured his life-long imagination. Once we realize César's mathematical-logic, that is, the social meaning of his logic, his way of knowing math and the manner in which he applied it to real-world social issues, we can understand an important intersection focusing on how it is that social change is possible both inside and outside the world of math. Thinking about math as a logic will help us experience the process of social change and how it is applicable to how we teach, learn and formulate math (as a formulaic calculus) from other ways of knowing, what we will call the "social calculus" of César Chávez in everyday life.

César's focus was always on the people. Again, when reflecting on the grape boycott he said:

It's not about the grapes it's about the people.

And,

Take out the grapes and put the focus on the people!

Concomitantly, when we apply César's superlative logic or that of "César the mathematician," he would suggest that when teaching and/or learning math we:

Take out the math and focus on the people.

This point cannot and should not be taken lightly as it goes to the core of how César would like for people to experience math. The shift in focus allows for a new way of knowing mathematics with a new focus, hence, a new paradigm for looking. Equipped with this new lens, let's peel back years of pedagogical behavior that has only focused primarily on the math and not the people. Upon doing so one of the first things we notice is that, much like César, our vernacular begins to change; now we are going to analyze things like the "calculus of a situation" and again turn our focus on the people (not the math), as César puts it, "Any problem we approach requires a group effort."

Looking at both the similarities and dissimilarities between the social and the formulaic usages of numbers we see its logical functions and limits, and as in calculus itself, we begin to reveal the social applications of differentiation, optimization, integrals and techniques of integration; recognizably these are the primary components behind the logic of mathematics, calculus and César's thinking. And by the way, the scientific community has been well aware of this logic for years; they simply are not well-versed at conveying and/or sharing it, especially not to Latino students interested in STEM fields. This is why it is so important to promote both cross-disciplinary and interdisciplinary approaches to teaching and learning math.

César saw math as both math and logic. For instance, when sitting on the stage at rallies he would look out over the crowds and guestimate how many people were in attendance by blocking off a section of the crowd in his mind and then using his visual block (say in blocks of 100 people) and "block out the crowd." César will be the first to admit that his estimates were always less than what news reporters reported. In his mind, this wasn't a bad thing; it was simply using logic to perform a mathematical function.

During César's time, the Texas Instruments Corporation was producing very smart hand-held calculators, and like many people his age he felt like it was no longer necessary to learn old school math like the rudiments of division and multiplication. Put differently, while he did feel strongly about learning the logic behind math, he did not feel strongly about having to learn all basic mathematical formulas in order to learn math– there is a major difference. Take for example, applying the popular statistical software known as "SPSS" (Statistical Packages for the Social Sciences),widely used for a variety of reasons, which measures the rates of an endless amount of statistical phenomenon (death, suicide, disease, human interests, divorce, political views, etc.)

In César's mind, it was important to understand the logic behind the numbers (i.e., statistics) but it was not necessary to learn high level statistics. This is a good analogy to the state of mathematics in this country today: some people believe it is important to learn statistics as part of operating SPSS while others do not; current research shows that it doesn't make a difference and the outcome is the same. The problem is that people who downplay learning math did not support the idea of learning to apply the logic behind math as did César.

The "mathemagician" Arthur Benjamin, a professor of mathematics at Harvey Mudd College, talks about the purpose of mathematics as three-fold: calculation, application and inspiration, which are the essence of César's idea of "social calculus." He would certainly agree with Professor Benjamin and add that we also need to deepen the inspiration of Latinos in all STEM fields. I can hear César say, "What if we looked at math differently?" We are here adopting César's logic to create a "social calculus" based again on the logic that "It's not about the math, it's about the people." This postulate causes a cognitive shift in one's thinking about math from a different perspective.

What if math was all about the people? César's logic gave birth to the idea of a "social calculus" where we focus more on the behavior of the people than we do the math and subsequently learn the math. Now César would turn this into a utilitarian calculus to be sure and search for ways to measure the consequences of social calculus. His logic coupled with Arthur Benjamin's notion, "Math is not just solving for X; it is also figuring out 'why'?" is the sort of thinking that causes a cognitive shift in such a manner that we come to see math quite differently. I have provided a few examples of this below as the basis for the creation of a new STEM "cell" for the purposes of deepening inspiration for those studying mathematics and also interested in the Latino imagination. There is an opportunity to observe where math is all about the people and where we can "not just solve for X" but also figure out "why" and that is in the case of Cuba. Now that's a real calculus, not just a formula but a theorem for awakening our brutish creativity a la Hobbes.

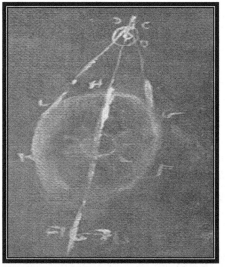

From painting by Gabriella Borges

Conversely, César used to joke and say that sometimes you have to "take out the people." He once heard about a mathematician who won a 1 million dollar prize for figuring out an equation that hadn't been solved in two years. As it turned out the mathematician was a recluse, lived out in the woods with little contact with other mathematicians, and this is why César argued he was able to find a solution to the equation, because he "took out the people" and solved it on his own accord. You might say César felt this way sometimes as well, taking his own plausibility and thus becoming only more plausible.

When you actually "take out the math and put in the people," the logic that remains is the logic César wants us to adapt: it is and it isn't mathematics in the popular sense, but talk to anyone earning a Ph.D. in mathematics and they will tell you that in their final years of study what they really focus on is logic, not pure numbers, and that's César's point: this is "social calculus." In short, what César presents is very much in line with the scientific method; his is a world view that helps us see a new logic of science, a new logic of how to think about STEM through a new paradigm for looking at this important effort to raise our nation's abilities in said fields. It's a paradigm that more than takes into account people's culture and addresses how we might better explain, that is, state in new ways of knowing, social problems and reveal the realities of conflict as problems of explanation or communication.

We need to develop a culture of social inquiry, encouraging research predicated on human behavior while teaching and learning math. In the case of teaching and learning mathematical concepts, César Chávez would have said, "We need to take out the math and put in the people," especially as we apply social scientific ethnographic field methods in online bilingual/bi-national settings. Again, if mathematicians themselves can take out the math when training new mathematicians, then logically speaking we can also take out the math for developing similar logics. Mihály Csíkszentmihályi, the founder of positive psychology, would agree and argue that mathematics can also be subjective, imagine that: passing beyond the vicissitudes of chance and entering a "flow"-like state of mind. The problem is most people never have the opportunity to wrap their heads around the idea of math in this way. César saw math as a mixture of the simpleminded and the unexpectedly complex; he knew these two things could coexist. His genius is grounded in a perverse consequence of his human condition. On the one hand he was fighting for better working/living conditions for farm workers, and he was supported by thousands of people. And on the other hand he was experiencing rapid personal self-transformation. These two factors led him to great insight and ingenuity when faced with everyday behaviors. To many, César was viewed as a genius.

This is a clear example of how César's values and beliefs have and continue to impact the Latino American psyche, how he inculcated his values and how they have shaped who we are and what we stand for. César has left his footprint on every special project I have initiated, for example, in writing a powerful vision statement for a brand new university in Monterey County. I found myself adding ideas such as, "serving educationally underserved populations of the State of California." Most especially as we were writing this statement and at the same time reeling from the effects of César's passing, fresh in our minds, we were reminded of César's emphasis on education for all, but especially for educationally underserved populations.

From painting by Gabriella Borges

Power and Knowledge

So what is the power in the knowledge of learning how calculus can be redesigned (pedagogically) to entice Latinos to learn mathematics and at the same time innovate by applying it in their research? Let me draw an analogy to Plato's "Allegory of the Cave." Plato's use of puppetry against the backdrop of an open flame allowing him to cast large shadows on a wall for prisoners to be observed from respective vantage points as they were chained to different parts of a cave, allowed Plato a unique platform (allegory) for describing how it is we come to develop a sense of reference for interpreting the world. Concomitantly, what I have referred to as "César's Social Calculus" is predicated on the unique nature of César's logic, that is, his sense of reference when he speaks about the lettuce strike: "It's not about the lettuce, it's about the people." In this case, if we examine César's logic more closely from a mathematical logical perspective, it's not about the lettuce or the people, it's about César's logic stemming from his sense of reference.

I might also add it was our ability to interpret and reinterpret what César said that added to the shaping of his Self in a social psychological sense and shaped him into a charismatic character and attractive as a leader. This is another way of saying that in American society we are always thinking about how to better improve upon how mathematics is taught, especially at the K through 12 grades. In the 1990s, I was working in the State of Texas and observed that the strategy for improving upon science and math was to couch ideas within Essential Elements. The idea was to cover the Essential Elements at the cost of all other "elements" less important.

Today, in American society we promote the idea of the Common Core as a means of standardizing what young students need to know, how they learn and how we might innovate on instructional approaches for teaching, which is, of course, César's sense of reference and starting point. César would not refer to this as a crisis in modern day mathematics, because his sense of reference is not crisis driven, rather he would begin by suggesting alternate approaches for all to benefit.

César shared meaning with the critical theorist Michael Foucault (*L'archéologie du savoir*, 1969) inasmuch as he understood:

> *The "relationship between power and knowledge, and how the former is used to control and define the latter. What authorities claim as 'scientific knowledge' are really just means of social control."*
> *Phillip Stokes, Philosophy: 100 Essential Thinkers.*

Similarly, when César's words are heard by a diverse group of people they are heard and translated quite differently. Some people take César's famous adage, "¡Si se puede!" (actually first presented by Doña Dolores Huerta) at one level and others do not take it lightly because it depends on the syntax of "¡Si se puede!" means one thing at one level, but if we change it slightly to "¡Si se puede, si se, si se puede!" it has the same meaning but at two varied levels. Some people hear the first and some people hear it with a slightly different meaning. For some, César's adage "¡Si se puede!" is inviolable, so changing it to "¡Si se puede, si se, si se puede!" some would argue changes the meaning. I would argue, however, that understanding César's sense of reference would make it discursively meaningful.

We find the same sort of logic applied to the symbolic logic of mathematics: to add 2+2 to get 4 is widely acceptable and laid out in a logic revered by non-mathematicians; in other words, the logic is untouchable because it is understandable, it has shared meaning, but to say 8-4+10-10 equals 4 would make the non-mathematicians uncomfortable. Each pathway equating to 4 is correct.

César and Doña Dolores shared meanings about numbers; however, their procedures were different from what the philosopher Jurgen Habermas calls "dialectical procedures" for obtaining the same outcome. The saying "¡Si se puede!" emerged at a time in this country's history when there was a fast growing underclass that the majority of society did not have contact with; they were the farm workers, people who worked hard in sometimes unspeakable conditions, in terrible housing and with no health benefits. So again the saying, "¡Si se puede!" caught on in the American Southwest but in reality resonated in two ways; this is only a minor example of Heintz' question, "Can mathematical meaning allow cultural analysis?"

"¡Si se puede!"

Reference: Heintz, C. "Can mathematical meaning allow cultural analysis?" in *Travelling Concepts II: Frame, Meaning, and Metaphor*, 2002).

Chapter Fifteen:

Saved by the Bell: Lift the Embargo, Learn New Ways of Lifting Mathematical Competencies

It is common knowledge that Cuban children are well-versed in mathematics and science; some are even selected for medical school training in the 8th grade, for Pete's sake. While the embargo against Cuba persists, we need to figure out the mindsets of compromise so as to find a means looking through César Chávez's paradigm for examining the field of education to find an important starting point in the STEM movement.

In theorizing César Chávez, we delve into the meaning of what impacts the embargo had on such things as teaching and learning math. One outcome of lifting the embargo would be the "marriage" of old-school communism and capitalism and how this plays out when it comes to learning math. At first glance, this may sound to many as absurd; it does so because we have to separate paradigms for looking at how math "gets done:" our visions for teaching and learning appear worlds apart–even beginning such a dialog is a bit uncanny.

To those who study the bench work of mathematicians, however, it becomes a question central to their topic of social inquiry. They find themselves asking, as Heintz did, "Can mathematical meaning allow cultural analysis?" (Heintz, C. *Travelling Concepts II: Frame, Meaning, and Metaphor*, 2002). So if compromises are to be met in lifting the embargo, we first need to realize the many impacts this will have on the emergence of new ideas in STEM fields and the transformation of Cuba and world culture because it will happen, and do so without encouraging further political polarization; César Chávez would agree.

The realities of lifting the embargo would certainly reveal a tangled process as neither country has the experience of undoing such a peculiar and long-standing phenomenon; all we know is that the situation has been uncompromising for decades and a good deal of mistrust has been generated between our two countries. The broad picture most analysts will focus on, of course, will be the political economic impacts like the "McDonaldization" of Cuba to include new economies, currency exchanges and the idea of credit, income, branding, mass marketing and the like. The point is that within the realm of education, the impacts of "normalization" are far less obvious, but remain just as important.

To say the "McDonaldization" of something has a rather negative connotation, one that current Cuban leaders would reject. Cynics will assume the worst, but it's the lens political economists will be using. For many, it's simply a paradigm for looking. The logical analogy is this: it's difficult to imagine Fidel Castro dressed up like Ronald McDonald, but it's much easier to envision Ronald McDonald dressed up like Fidel Castro. Actually it depends on one's definition or what you mean by the "McDonaldization" of Cuba– which is not necessarily low wages and tedious work, a development César Chávez would oppose, of course. However, César may favor the mission of McDonald's, which is "to serve the customer, and if you are not serving the customer, then you are serving the person who is serving the customer."

In theorizing César Chávez, let's raise a few questions that get to the core of our quest to lift STEM competencies:

- What was it about the embargo as a societal experience that had a positive impact on teaching, learning and pedagogy in Cuba?
- As evidenced by the ongoing operation of pop-cultural 60 and 70 year-old vehicles in daily life, did the embargo create a 'can do' atmosphere in the behavior of Cubanos? Is this why they "can do" math so well?
- What do we have to learn from their pedagogical approaches, especially in STEM fields?
- What role does ideology play in teaching and learning?
- Can mathematical meaning allow cultural analysis?
- What insights might we gain by researching how we might spark the mathematical imagination of Latinos? Hence, what is there to be discovered about Cuban-Latino to U.S.-Latino pedagogy?

In his later years, César Chávez would have raised such questions about lifting the embargo because for him it was all about the people (his leadership is certainly sorely needed at this time). By raising insightful questions, César had the uncanny ability to cause cognitive shifts in our thinking about situations. Somewhere between his humor and superlative logic and ponderings on lifting the embargo, he once observed:

> *Once the embargo is lifted, the island of Cuba will come out of the water some ten feet or more and new ideas will be revealed and begin to spawn like never before!*

Toward the end of his life, César's influence was spreading world-wide. Cuban leadership would be a seismic mismatch against César: he fought for civil rights and Cuban leaders have made it clear–oppression reigns. This clash between our cultures will cause sacrifices on all sides. Beyond his belief in civil rights, however, César did not believe in creating an extractive structure of Cuban society.

If he were with us today and in the capacity of an Ambassador of Good Will, through his powerful ideas alone, César would cause a social movement and get involved in "inCUBAndoing." His ideas would complement our thinking in readying our two countries for more access, and his insightful questions could only cause a positive and sparkling interchange of binational ideas. In relation to the STEM movement and again matching his wit, superlative logic and humor, he would suggest the creation of STEM "cells," specific to all types of research and suggest we "inCUBAte" them according to each respective field: science, technology, engineering and mathematics.

César would certainly see in lifting the embargo against Cuba an opportunity that should not be taken lightly; he understood that due to their forced deprivation, Cubans have a long history of innovative pedagogical training in the STEM fields, demonstrated by their high level of research and world-class advancements in medicine and medical research. The outcome of such an ideology could only improve upon scientific inquiry in the United States and benefit Latino learners as well. Once the island of Cuba starts "coming out of the water," as César puts it, new ideas about teaching and learning will be realized, no matter how peculiar they may appear to U.S. observers.

Saved by the Bell

At the outset of the Cuban Revolution, then President and Dictator Fidel Castro declared there would be no religions in Cuba, especially no Christianity; it was a symbolic gesture against all oppressors, namely Spanish conquistadores. For Fidel, even the sound of a bell from a church tower was sending an oppressive message to all of those within ear-shot, so in his capacity as a dictator he outlawed bells from daily usage, that is to say, "all bells." A by-product of this act was the historical persistence and cultural belief held by many Cubans that bells are inherently bad for society, so they were never installed in institutions, businesses, or any public spaces. The point is that Cuban students in grades K through 12 do not measure the end of a class by the sounding of a bell. Psychologically speaking, there is no bell to trigger a pleasurable release of dopamine to the brain and cause habitual behavior, namely, running out of class at the sound of the bell. Fidel Castro has argued that pedagogically, bells are only disruptive just as they are to the psyche of a society and the development of the Self (in a social psychological sense) in individuals; Freud would agree.

In Cuban schools, no matter what a student's class schedule is they are "not allowed" to leave their math class (nor do they want to) until everyone in the class demonstrates they have learned the lesson for the day. It should be noted that having to stay in class until everyone understands and can demonstrate their mastery of the lesson for the day is not viewed as a punishment, as it is in the United States; rather, it is looked upon as an achievement, a group effort, a symbolic badge of sorts, "We [the group] got it!"

One way to look at this situation is that, as Fidel Castro puts it, "It's all about outcomes!" Meet the outcome and you can go; that's what brings cultural meaning to mathematical analysis. In this light, it wasn't until the birth of the STEM Movement in American society that we began thinking about STEM subject matter (in this case mathematics) as a K through 16, (not just K through 12) challenge.

Photo by Armando A. Arias

U.S. students look forward to darting out of the classroom door just as soon as the bell rings, not thinking about whether or not what the teacher just 'taught' them to is relevant."

Just as soon as the hands of the clock trigger the bell dismissing them from class they dart out the door; even the good students do the same.

Conversely, in Cuba no matter what a student's class schedule is, there is no bell to respond to (no dopamine cheap thrill); this allows for a very different learning culture as students stay in class until the math problem is solved and everyone can demonstrate their mastery of the lesson of the day, one could argue that this behavior is tied directly to their ideology. When it comes to teaching and learning math, Cuban learning logic prevails.

What the Cubans figured out a long time ago was the lucid intellectual communion between habitual behavior and ideology, some call it "communistic teaching," as if to infer math for Communists only. Yet in the U.S. we now call it "group learning." What's the difference as long as the outcome is reached? It's called "learning math." Moreover, it doesn't make any sense to provide a lecture and take students on a mathematical journey, run the risk of making a mistake and not have time to repair the mistake, lead them into learning peril and then let them go when the bell rings.

Rather the idea is to stick with the problem until it is solved. You can see how learning math in Cuba derives cultural meaning and leads to behaviors that are tied to their cultural behavior (ideology) and why Cuban consciousness is predicated on a "can do" attitude. In short, the embargo has caused Cuban innovation in the teacher's bench work, having "to do" while doing without has inadvertently caused innovation, unlike in American society where we are habitually learned to be "saved by the bell." There are many U.S. math teachers who are doing a great job; they know well their own earnest quest for education, identity, and voice. At the same time, they have not lost their avidity for experience; they may even say to me, "What do you know? What are you talking about, you have never taught math?" And they are correct, but I have performed a good deal of systematic research in Cuba, directly observing how math teachers teach, and they have not.

In the example above you can also see how in the U.S. our pedagogy (capitalistic driven) takes into account less than hourly math lessons often filled with interruptions, disciplinary actions and administrative minutia. In Cuban schools there are far less disciplinary problems (almost none; it's simply not part of the classroom culture), so little time is spent on that issue. Because U.S. students "live by the bell," the subliminal psychological message we instill in our youth is that it is okay literally to put problem-solving off into the future due to some artificial dopamine drive time schedule. From a social psychological standpoint, time regulated behavior contributes to the shaping of the Self and human condition.

Castro saw this problem as a product of capitalism; in translation he views U.S. citizens as people who run away from their problems, preferring to "live by the bell," if you will. Castro views U.S. citizens as being raised by the bell and many go on to take jobs where they have to punch a clock (yet another form of bell ringing).

This is a good point and provides evidence for why it is that U.S. students come to hate math the way they do and how this plays out for the rest of their lives.

In this way, Castro does not buy into the popular adage "saved by the bell" as the bell only excuses people from the situation, hence, from reaching the outcomes that are clearly stated at the outset. Living life without a bell in this way becomes a classic example of how math "gets done" in a communist society; call it "communistic math" if you will, call it whatever you want--there are lessons to be learned from such pedagogical behaviors not practiced in the U.S. and this is what we must at the same time watch for and encourage when teaching and learning opportunities rise up as the embargo is lifted. This is why Professor Arthur Benjamin's postulate "X equals why" is very deep.

When we come to understand "why," deeper levels of predication and/or endless forms of teaching and learning are discovered due to the successful "marriage" of our contrasting paradigms for learning math. We will inevitably rise to new levels of mathematical insight; our mathematical imagination will be continuously sparked, from actually understanding math to how math "gets done" and its applications.

In the spirit of César Chávez we have to ask "Why do students in the U.S. have to leave class at the sound of a bell?" It's difficult to argue that living by the bell or having bells in instructional settings is a good pedagogical design, yet it is truly part of U.S. culture and one could argue that there is a capitalistic drive behavior in need of critical examination as above. As shown by our brief analysis, asking "Why?" moves the focus of learning math, off math onto the people which can be very telling and again, create new ways of knowing, math, a la Cubano. This is what is missing from our approaches to teaching and learning in STEM fields. In short, while learning the traditional standards that form the basis for STEM fields, we must also move beyond traditional teaching and learning, set competency-based goals, and reach our outcomes. Why? Because it's all about outcomes!

From painting by Gabriella Borges

Lifting the embargo will inevitably lead to new ways of learning math and lifting STEM competencies: bringing cultural meaning to mathematical analysis and mathematical meaning to cultural analysis.

Given this insight César Chávez would encourage us to delve deeper into teaching and learning math Cubano-style and to search for solutions to problems people don't know they have, in turn improving upon our math competency in the U.S. Why do we teach math the way we do in the U.S.? Presently there is a major movement in the U.S. for instilling a Common Core, a set of national standards for teaching and learning that has no room for new and innovative pedagogical approaches as described above (and in the chapters to follow). Why don't we take into account other ways of knowing and other ways of learning, such as how we can learn from our own mistakes? Now this will get us on the road to a new cultural voraciousness as the Island of Cuba "comes out of the water" and begins to reveal the truth about their highly successful approaches to teaching and learning math. Que viva matemática!

Chapter Sixteen:

Truly Learning from Our Mistakes – Our Mathematical Mistakes

Isn't it ironic that in American society we promote the idea of learning from our mistakes, yet when learning math we only want to learn from part of our mistakes and not from all of our mistakes. Read on. Psychologically speaking, students in the U.S. are self-selective about choosing which of their mathematical mistakes to address, due for the most part to practical reasons.

Teachers and professors alike take points off for parts of mathematical equations and not off the entire assessment of the equation. Similarly, in a classroom setting math teachers are selective as well because they pick-and-choose mistakes by students that can convey a broad learning lesson to learn from the problem. This is especially the case when it comes to learning math. What math instructors know and grapple with on a daily basis is that we all have different learning styles, sometimes radically different; we also have different styles for making mistakes.

Take the case of Cuba, which has endured an embargo by the U.S. for a half century, but now boasts the highest number per capita of classic and vintage U.S.-made automobiles in the world. What is more remarkable is that somehow they're still running. Truth is, an embargo works both ways, preventing the exchange of ideas about how best to teach young people mathematics or any subject for that matter.

In Cuba's schools, an effective pedagogical strategy for learning math is for students and teachers alike to focus on everyone's mathematical mistakes, particularly when the mistake started, when it was actually made and how individuals go about trying to repair their mistakes. Said differently, Cuban students are expected to focus on how it is they actually made mathematical mistakes as compared with their peers and this becomes a topic for mathematical inquiry for the entire class to engage in for the entire term.

Politically, some U.S. citizens would call this "socialistic" and somehow define it as "evil." Mathematicians in the U.S. would call it "math." Truth be told, no matter where you are from on the planet, math-is-math even when it is politicized; it is a symbolic approach to communication across cultures (primitive or not). Math is used to convey both simple and complex ideas; to a large extent, it is a universal language. Given this social fact, it is more absurd to differentiate between types of math, whether they are founded in democratic or socialistic societies than it is to talk about pedagogical strategies–again, math-is-math!

Because math-is-math, let's focus on mathematical mistakes as a shared reference point for meaning between Cuban and U.S. cultures. When it comes to teaching and learning mathematics, our common enemy in math is the fact that we all make mathematical mistakes. Think about it this way: we all have had the experience of sitting in a math class where the teacher will describe an equation or fundamental theorem of calculus, like The Chain Rule, lecture for the better part of an hour and then suddenly stop, look up at the class and say something like, "Oh my god, that's incorrect! Forget everything I just said, it's all wrong!" and then suddenly the bell rings and everyone runs out the door.

Whether the information you were just exposed to is correct or incorrect, you can't possibly forget everything the teacher just explained, you may even remain perplexed until the next class, suspended existentially, caught in a web of contradictions or you may never really learn the materials and drop the class as a result; correct or incorrect it's still difficult to unlearn what you were just "taught." This happens all the time, perhaps more often than you think. It doesn't matter if the mathematical mistake was made by the teacher or the student, the pedagogy Cuban school children are exposed to examines the *act of the mistake* as a tool for learning and sparking the mathematical imagination.

Imagine if we took such an approach in U.S. schools. We might find STEM learning and performance skyrocket. Said differently, the nature and analysis of mathematical mistakes (made on the spot) become the curriculum. It's just like César's idea of *social calculus*:

Cuban students are taught first to "bracket" (identify) the mistake, take a closer look at when the mistake started, analyze how the mistake was made and also take a close look at how the teacher tried to repair the mistake. In social scientific terms one might say, "We identify the situation (mistake), define its *situatedness* (how the mistake is repaired), thus presenting the cultural meaning of the outcome (methodology) and its theoretical framework (mathematical meaning).

In this sense there can be no standards, no Common Core, as we define it in the U.S., because learning is viewed as highly *situational*, much like every day social life. When it comes to math and its application, the Cuban philosophy is that "it depends on the situation." Given endless combinations of mathematical formulas, integers, equations and the like, each combination gives rise to the *situatedness of numbers*, in short, what we learn depends on the mistakes we make or present, yet what we learn is grounded in real numbers, most often in real situations.

The problem with situated learning (Freud would argue) in the U.S. is that the *ego* gets in the way, because we live in a society that does not readily own up to admitting to and/or facing our immediate mistakes. He would say we "place blame for our mistakes, elsewhere, but certainly not within ourselves." He would further state that the *ego* really has only one true chance to admit having made a mistake at the exact time the act of the mistake occurred. If not immediately admitted, the mistake will take on the form of secondary elaborations along with other distractions to avoid self-admission and the mistake will become masked with illusions.

Academics outside of the U.S. have observed that, especially in the United States, teachers and professors are egocentric because that is the way they are trained, as Freud would suggest. As a direct result, they would find it hard to admit they have made a mistake in public (in a classroom) and try to work around repairing their mistakes rather than address the mistake itself. It's no wonder we have created what Freud calls a "civilization of discontents" (*Civilization and Its Discontents*).

A singular example of the manifestation of this idea can be grounded in the instance of a third grade math teacher in San Diego, California, who was observed making this statement while drawing analogies to math. "The Rocky Mountains are hundreds and hundreds of miles high" only to be corrected by her student who had once lived in Denver who blurted out "But teacher how can that be? Denver is only a mile high." The student recognized the teacher's mistake, yet became immediately embarrassed, because in American society we are led to believe that teachers don't make many mistakes. In turn the teacher scolded and shamed the child in front of his classmates for having corrected her; at the same time, she never acknowledged the fact that she was incorrect, nor did she correct her mistake. The situation became all about the student correcting the teacher and not about the math.

The young student reported the incongruity of his teacher's statement, that the "Rocky Mountains are hundreds and hundreds of miles high" to his parents and wanted clarification from them as he truly wanted to know what he had done wrong. When his parents asked him what he had said to his teacher that made him so upset, he told them and started to cry, inadvertently revealing the *degradation ceremony* the teacher had put him through in front of his peers. The teacher was subsequently confronted by the boy's parents. Still, the mathematical incongruity was again left unaddressed and the "problem" of the young student's behavior was placed squarely on the table. Moreover, the focus was taken off the teacher's mistake and placed on the "misconduct" of the third grader. They never got back to solving the problem that was mathematical in nature.

This reinforces the notion that we have an ego-based teaching culture and as a result many teachers in the U.S. do not take ownership of their mistakes and in turn inadvertently make up excuses for their mistakes. This is what Freud would say we are teaching our students, even in math classes; it's not about the math, it is about the "misconduct" (a student correcting the teacher). The teacher is discontented and her pedagogical approach is being impacted by this manifestation and will continue to be over her career causing deep levels of negative psychological impact.

In K through 12 grades in American society, Freud, recognizing this pedagogical contradiction, would argue that because we hesitate to admit our mistakes, what we have is a restless aspiration for a more meaningful life. You might say that this is one of the greatest contributions of the Cuban Revolution. Ideology and pedagogy are linked in this way; any Common Core element up for discussion during the lifting of the embargo would include literally learning from one's mistakes–it's the unspeakable truth.

It's so common to learn from one's mistakes (not just give lip service to the idea) that it is assumed that everyone will do so in an open and soothing learning atmosphere. Freud's analysis is deep because what he is saying in short is that when you leave the ego outside of the classroom, real learning begins and this is what the Cubans learned a long time ago. Conversely, in American society the ego is the first thing to enter the room; don't forget, the "Rocky Mountains are hundreds and hundreds of miles high!!!" Why? "Because I said so!" says the third grade teacher.

Many teachers in the U.S. continue to see themselves as the *fountain of knowledge.* In this case, the ego is misconstrued and gets in the way of teaching, learning and the self-development of teachers and students alike. Said differently, the ego is a very difficult thing to transform; it would take a deep therapeutic process to transfer values related to going from a fountain of knowledge mentality to something else. In other words, first we have to get teachers in the U.S. in the habit of admitting their mistakes when teaching. Then we have to make their mistakes apparent by identifying and analyzing their mistakes followed by creating a curriculum built on truly learning from one's mistakes. In addition there is the problem of teachers who simply don't know their subject matter as we find many times in the cases where physical education coaches are asked to teach math classes in order to fill up their workload. A lot of bad information can be transferred in such a setting, yet it occurs in American society, but in Cuba it is simply not allowed.

Ego aside, U.S. math teachers all have very different teaching styles to be sure but they use the same common materials to teach from. This being the case, math teachers make mistakes at different points, some will realize they are making mistakes immediately while others will go on for several minutes, well into their mistakes. Focusing on the manner in which math teachers repair their mistakes, perhaps even categorizing them, ala *Cubano* style, is the way math teachers in American society may discover once the embargo is fully lifted and can integrate creative thinking into their own bench work. Our STEM students stand to benefit from all similar pedagogical situations. To be sure this "discovery" will be hailed as fascinating, but what will be even more fascinating from a social psychological perspective is when we begin sharing the mistakes with U.S. math teachers who made them.

In the absence of Google or Google Scholar, young Cubans are taught to pause, rethink and reimagine what they are learning on the spot; psychologically speaking they do not mix ego with learning as we do in the U.S. This is an important point because a huge amount of poor teaching and bad information is being distributed as a direct result of ego-centric behavior.

This point cannot and should not be taken lightly as Cuban culture teaches children to admit their mistakes at every opportunity, which takes us back to Freud's idea about first having to admit your mistake to yourself and take immediate ownership of it from the onset. The pedagogy practiced in Catholic schools in the early 20th century was to slap or strike students with rulers when they made a mistake. Cuban math teachers don't have to grapple with all the psychological trauma or stress generated when they make a mistake and one might argue that this makes for improved teaching as well as better teacher bench work.

Degrading a student for correcting a teacher is equivalent to striking them and could provide some level of trauma, never to be forgotten. Conversely, in Cuban schools it is impossible to deny a mistake (nor would one want to) as reexamination and analysis of mistakes is viewed as a group effort, a collective behavior for the good of the whole. From a pedagogical standpoint, the good thing that comes out of pointing out mistakes made by the teacher and/or student is how the dialog shifts from denying they made mistakes to how to better repair the mistakes to how to collaborate with groups of students to learn math from their mistakes.

This is a classic example of César Chavez's idea of a "social calculus" as well as one we can add as a method for learning math. Along these lines of logic, Freud might suggest that we "take out the ego, reshape it, and put it back in again." Moreover by examining mathematical mistakes in this way we make learning math *social*, we "take out the math and put in the people" just as César would advise, and the outcome is that we would have not only a new way of viewing a mathematical problem, but now we would do so *multi-perspectively*, learning at the same time both math as well as the "calculus of the situation."

Once realized, the subliminal by-product of lifting the embargo (metaphorically for the time being) in terms of teaching and learning is the potential to have a deep impact on the psyche of American society inasmuch as people within the realm of the STEM fields are longing for improved methods for teaching but do not have the tools nor the mathematical imagination to do so even when they are often told to "think-out-of-the-box," but like a pet kitten are taught to "not go outside the box" the litter box, that is.

The window for making pedagogical observations about how math, as well as other areas of STEM fields, is taught in Cuba will be short as everything about the island nation is already changing, including teaching and learning. Below are some suggestions from yet an unchanged Cuban teaching situation based on the study of mistakes.

From the perspective of César Chavez's *social calculus* when it comes to teaching and learning math we need to develop STEM "cells" that foster a culture of social inquiry and innovation, encouraging research predicated on human behavior while teaching and learning math (and other STEM fields). As shown by these few examples, lifting the embargo would undoubtedly reveal new ways of lifting STEM competencies and at the same time spark the mathematical imagination of teachers and students alike as we may infuse and/or adopt the following Cuban pedagogical strategies for improved teaching and learning in math:

- Identify issues surrounding learning, such as how does a teacher "un-teach" what he just taught the class, because he made a mistake.
- Create a science of examining mathematical mistakes and how to repair them, that is, thus creating the art and science of learning by mistakes.
- Create groups to identify mistakes and patterns of mistakes.
- Create groups to undo the mistakes and correct them in a presentation format to the class, immediately following the mistake.

Concomitantly, in Cuba students demonstrated that:

- They learn math more thoroughly by examining mistakes made by their teachers and fellow students.
- They learn by close examination of the mistakes teachers make during lecture.
- They come to have a more improved relationship with both the teachers and other students.
- Apprentice teachers come to see their craft in an innovative manner in terms of how it will impact their personal bench work.

And, Cuban teachers report that they:

- Are made aware of instructional behaviors they did not know existed.
- Become better "repairers" of their mathematical mistakes.
- They come to view themselves as both the *subject* and the *object* during course lectures and this helps them create an open learning environment.

Doesn't this way of knowing math leave the indelible impression that *social calculus* may lead to a spike in innovation and expand the mathematical imagination? As Albert Einstein put it, "Imagination is more important than knowledge."

Through the study of mathematical mistakes, using the Cuban model, we create the opportunity in a soothing learning environment to explain one's thought process to others, significant others (classmates) if you will, while at the same time working collaboratively, all trying to reach the same outcome or to learn math. In calculus, this is referred to as "optimization," which is very similar to opportunity theory in the social sciences. Cuban students have demonstrated a liberated behavior that is the outcome of the psychological therapy derived from describing their thought process, a nice by-product to be sure.

SECTION 6

Chapter Seventeen:

César Defined Spatiality and Public Spaces for Social Protest: The Birth of the Real Space Program

César Chávez discovered during the famous United Farmer Worker (UFW) March from Delano to Sacramento (1966) that many townships did not allow public parades (certainly not protest marches) in the middle of the street without a permit. Thus, at the onset of the march from Delano they were confronted with a Sheriff demanding a permit. César's immediate response was to have everyone walk on the sidewalks, for him it was a no brainer; it would have taken me a month to figure this out, but César figured it out on the spot.

This act was yet another demonstration of César's superlative logic and it didn't stop there: it was a moment in the history of the UFW Movement when all at once (just like a scientific discovery), Mexican farm workers and Chicanos experienced spatial and discursive entitlement, it was as they say, a game changer because this incident caused them (as well as observers) to see public space in new ways and an era of reclamation and discontent began as people who never owned property discovered a new-found feeling in "owning" public space no matter how brief, with or without a permit. Whoa! In the analysis of the UFW Movement, its initiation of political acts and spatial entitlements is an important topic for social inquiry.

Although she does not discuss the UFW Movement specifically, the idea of *discursive entitlement* is described within this context by Gaye Theresa Johnson, an acolyte of postmodern theorists, in her book, *Spaces of Conflict, Sounds of*

Solidarity: Music, Race, and Spatial Entitlement in Los Angeles (2013), "...as a synonym for the adaptive, ideological, subjective, stylized, or symbolic assertion of power." In all his brilliance, César's technique of placing conflicts between farmers and UFW members and supporters in this way caused a shift away from the rhetoric of only spatial entitlement, which, of course, became the thinking that turned that rhetoric on its head.

When César Chávez and the United Farm Workers first began organizing people in the agricultural fields, the first thing the farmers did was to threaten them with guns and rifles claiming they were "trespassing" on private property; farmers claimed their use of force was legitimate because they were "defending their land." In addition, local law enforcement was called in and UFW organizers were escorted, handcuffed and pushed off private properties at gun point. As Fred Ross, lead UFW organizer once put it, "Shots always seemed to be fired; it always felt like a stand-off, but only one side had guns and it wasn't us!"

Farmers had long experienced spatial entitlement in their lands, passed on from one generation to the next so the idea of "their land" had been ingrained in them since before they were born into a world of entitlement. It's no wonder farmers saw the actions of the UFW as "trespassing." They were tapados (close–minded) because their view of what was "rightfully" theirs was being challenged and their assumptions about what was theirs had never been challenged.

César introduced different discursive entitlement rhetoric unlike that of the rhetoric of spatial entitlement farmers had used at least up to this point. César's powerful rhetoric melded legalities and human rights in a nonviolent manner that challenged farmers' understanding about what was theirs. César introduced a new discursive entitlement rhetoric specific to the human rights of Mexican farm workers. Said differently, no one had ever presented human rights in the way César did and many social movement groups began observing UFW action strategies, which in turn attracted many non-Latinos to the UFW Movement. César exposed the values and beliefs as well as the myths farmers had passed on for generations. At every step, he exposed their oppressive management habits and behaviors by which they had created a form of modern-day slavery, which they would not define as such, but which certainly had all the characteristics of slavery. César had lifted the veil of objectivity for the world to see and what was revealed was a form of modern-day slavery and exploitation taken to new heights both knowingly and unknowingly constructed by farmers addicted to maximizing their profits at the cost of human rights and dignity. It didn't take farmers long to ascertain that César was initiating a political act, however, as he put it, "They didn't know what hit them!" In this way César became to social change science what Einstein became to particle physics science and that was, simply stated. a genius! Que viva César Chávez!

What Fred Ross inadvertently discovered while in confrontation with local authorities who were ordering UFW organizers off the farms because they were on private property was that there was land–space between farms and public access roads and highways which the farmers did not own–the space between where farms end and where public space begins is, in fact, public domain space, in essence the space where farm workers park their cars to work the fields. Coming to this realization, César and Fred began promoting the idea that there are interstitial zones on every farm and UFW organizers, members and supporters, had every right to be on public land to organize and carry their message.

Farmers realized as well that many of them had assumed that much of the land adjacent to farms was actually theirs, so they often extended their fields, never communicating this to the next generations who then, of course, unknowingly defended "their" land with guns and rifles. Although this was only a spatial entitlement issue for the UFW, imagine what a huge problem erupted during the gold rush days. When people with official U.S. Government permits often discovered gold on a boundary line of another permit holder—that led to confrontations, similarly to those between farmers and UFW organizers, in turn this often led to having to call in official surveyors who were often bribed and/or murdered over where boundaries were drawn, tough job.

It's important to note that during much of their earliest stages, not only the UFW Movement but also the Chicano Movement took place in public interstitial zones. Abiding by the law, Richard (César's brother) drove the flatbed truck they had converted into a mobile *altar* to the Virgin Mary along the public zones between the farms and the public roads in order to attract farm workers toiling in the fields on private property. Luis Valdez and the Teatro Campesino did the same, again a discovery that was simply brilliant and sent a powerful message to social change activists of the time.

We cannot take lightly what the spatial versus discursive logics brought to bear, a factor that has been overlooked by historians who have researched the UFW social movement. Competing logics found in the contradictions emanating from the new rhetoric being forged by conflicting world views caused a paradigm shift in the politics of the 1960s and 1970s, precipitating many new forms of social action as well as new competing logics. Psychologically speaking, the idea of public space available for public protest that exists in the "in between" was key to the birth of modern-day social movement consciousness.

On the one hand, the farmers could see the world only through the eyes of spatial entitlement and on the other the UFW and Chicano Movements were beginning to see the world through a new discursive entitlement as César was presenting; these were in fact competing paradigms for looking at the same situation. His rhetoric was as powerful as President John F. Kennedy's and together they contributed towards a consciousness that would forever change the thinking of future generations. Psychologically, these are distinct and problematic conflicting realities when placed in one situation.

It was the process of disambiguation of the word "space" that César knew he had to key in on to communicate ideas surrounding spatial versus discursive entitlement, especially when dealing with farmers who had strong feelings about the space they owned versus farm workers who had never owned space and did not have strong feelings about land ownership. From a social psychological perspective, you might say, for people who had never owned land, their feelings about how public space may be utilized are just as strong if not stronger than those who have had strong feelings about their private lands. In the early 1970s, for example, radical Chicanos knew local police officers did not respect their space (barrios) and often did not respond to 911 emergency calls so in turn Chicanos responded with, "Fuck the pigs, get them out of our community!" This is the point.

Moreover, during times when the UFW was organizing it became apparent that farmers had a real sense for spatiality, hence, they thought they knew exactly where their property lines were drawn; after all they are farmers and they want to make the most of their property and grow the biggest crops possible for profit-making reasons. For farmers, the idea of space and how many acres of land they own is commonplace; in California, the majority of the sons of these farmers attend "Cal Poly" (California Polytechnic State University located in San Luis Obispo) earning bachelors and masters level degrees in agricultural sciences. In other words, they learn how to manage and measure their land, learning formulas for how much seed to purchase, pesticides, gasoline, farm laborers, etc. In the past, farming knowledge was passed down from generation to generation; the modern day approach calls for offspring to learn farming techniques and methods at the university.

In university studies, the agricultural sciences curriculum promotes a paradigm for looking at one's property to maximize benefits. As you might expect, farmers have this ingrained in their heads, always searching for new ways of minimizing expenses and maximizing profits; it's no wonder farmers have traditionally sought out cheap labor to harvest their crops–you might call this a model for exploitation by curricular design.

Conversely, farm workers, especially those from Mexico, are enticed from Mexico to migrate to the U.S., no matter what financial or psychological toll it may take on the family. They simply develop a "go for it" attitude, all the while understanding that they may have to live and work under inhumane conditions. What César found early on in the UFW Movement was that the situation in the agricultural fields is certainly conflicted in the minds of those that worked the land. The glaring conflict was that there were those who owned what Karl Marx called the "means of production" and there were those "who worked the means of production." Together they had very different experiences on the same space on a daily basis. Farmers had a sense of spatiality learned both at the university and at home as a cultural entitlement allowing them to gain wealth and hand it down to future generations.

Farm workers were not born into a world where people were space conscious; they didn't think about buying land because they could never afford to nor did they ever have the means to pass land down to the next generation. The United Farm Workers as a "united front" were empowered to exert a new, more powerful and effective discursive entitlement towards improved working conditions, housing, wages and respect.

Because the UFW stood up to giant agribusinesses the way they did, a new-found form of spatiality lodged itself directly into the American psyche. This was one of the greatest contributions César Chávez made to the world and to tactics for social change. Spatiality as a concept and/or topic of social inquiry had not been popularized in the early 1960s when a number of social movements were materializing, yet community organizers and activists were taking to the streets (public spaces) in the form of public marches and this was transforming the consciousness of individuals to the point they felt empowered as never before. Empowerment related to spatiality took on forms of reclamation that people had not experienced before. Symbolically speaking, Mexican farm workers in the U.S. often display Mexican flags on a regular basis in honor of their heritage and Mexican Independence Day (September the 16th).

The early 1960s were an active time to disambiguate the word "space," as President John F. Kennedy was talking about expanding the space program and "placing a man on the moon," while Fidel Castro talked about the "ninety mile space between Cuba and Florida." Countries around the world began claiming international water space rights far out to sea, hippies for the first time talked about being "spaced-out." And the consciousness of several hundred farmers were being raised because the United States Government had taken over (occupied) space on their farms (averaging one hundred acres of space) in order to strategically place nuclear missile silos aimed at Cuba, along with fences and roads and a sentry station due to the threat and scare from the Cuban Missile Crisis. It was in this context during this time period (1960s–1970s) that the process of disambiguation of the word "space" had to be dealt with.

People began to think about themselves in terms of world events and global definitions in turn; this led to new feelings of alienation and to collective searches for identity and for space. To some extent the success of the UFW was all about timing. In the transformation of the American psyche, its membership swelled with supporters in search of their own identity and theirs was a great cause. Even in the world of technology (just prior to the Internet) with the advent of the Micro-Vax, the first computer main frame invented by the Digital Equipment Corporation, people were being introduced to altogether new concepts such as the meaning of "virtual space."

The point is that at the societal level, the process of disambiguation of the term "space" was taking its toll on the American psyche and this was not of César's concern; he didn't think about it in the same way as most. Rather he was focused on his need to help the farmers, farm workers, UFW members and supporters to understand that boundaries surrounding farms needed to be reexamined. This more than upset a lot of farmers and at the same time challenged the work of surveyors, calling into question whether or not malfeasance and misfeasance had occurred when defining property lines. The outcome? In nearly every case farmers over time had extended their property lines and by law property lines had to be redrawn. Even so, farmers, agitated to the core of their souls, defended the lands they thought were theirs. The world was watching César's strategic moves; his superlative logic was calling into question the idea of space in terms of land ownership, and in so doing led the way to new forms of social protest–in public space–and the real space program was born.

Armando A. Arias

Chapter Eighteen:

Suspended Existentially

César faced the same dilemma as did Socrates: he exposed the truth about social injustices as well as many policies having a negative impact on the human condition. Socrates exposed the oppressive political tactics of political leaders. César exposed a multitude of exploitive tactics employed by farmers. It didn't take long before farm workers came to understand him and the people in power wanted to shut him up!

I have applied César's philosophy and superlative logic and have taken true accounts and fictionalized them; I have also taken fictionalized accounts and reported them as non-fictional. This was César's scientific methodology for getting at the truth that scientists often sweep under the rug, keeping it hidden under a veil of objectivity. Within the realm of the scientific method, this contradiction is in fact the basis of all sciences. All theories start out as fiction: they are all dreamt up, that's why they're called, "theories." Without contradictions there would be no advancement in science and all scientists know this. Plato's idea behind the first Academy was predicated on this premise. Today's Academy of Sciences sees this as their mission.

This type of thinking is very telling about how César constructed his reality. It didn't matter if he were talking to someone, examining an event, experiencing a situation and/or thinking up a strategy, he knew that whatever he saw and/or experienced, others would see differently and he accepted this as the nature of the truth. He used to say in a philosophical tone, "The center will never hold!" and he was okay with that. César was driven by this logic.

To farm workers, he would say, "You are marginalized in the U.S. because..." and to the laborers of the world, "Our labor problems are the same as exploitive labor problems everywhere!" The truth in César's voice rang true everywhere! César was not a highly trained Western scientist, yet he didn't need a Ph.D. in science, technology, engineering or mathematics to see the changing nature of scientific truth. He was not a skeptic, he simply understood truth-seeking at a very deep and emotional level. Capturing, grounding, theorizing, and enjoying César's superlative logic and ideas is the premise of this work and the act of theorizing César Chávez.

César was in the midst of self-discovery prior to meeting an untimely death. He was, in fact, soul-searching, seeking inner-truths but was not yet far enough in his personal discovery process to make linkages to his outer and inner thoughts. César was not subject to a nervous disorder as some of his best critics suggest. He didn't show signs of anxiety, neurosis or hysteria, nor did he have any phobias. While serving in the U.S. Navy, he developed a slight fear of deep wide-open bodies of water (like most people) as he often jumped off the bottom deck of ships while they were anchored out at sea as part of his training. For him, swimming in the open sea was liberating much like having new thoughts, but it also made him realize he was not a strong swimmer and this contradiction caused him to think inward.

Concomitantly, he understood street smarts because he had to help his family survive with very little and it took creativity to do so. Sometimes people would refer to him as a "genius" and this caused him to reflect on his experiences as a child. For example, at one point his family was so poor that he and his brothers went out to the slaughter houses and would pile through cow patties (cow poop), pull out the beans, boil them up and eat them. And on other days, his mother would make chicken soup for several days straight using the same chicken. César would tell people these stories and then say, "If you want to call this genius, I want to call it survival; we had to think of ways to survive! Some might even call it, 'thinking outside-the-box.'" He wanted to excel in gaining more formal knowledge and this propelled the basis for his logic in seeking the meaning of his life.

As César became more introspective later in his life, he practiced more-and-more self-reflection and while searching for his innermost self he became much more pensive and spoke aloud much less than he had in his younger years. He was displaying shy behavior that was unlike him; you might say he was not the same-old

César of the 1960s. He would talk about the pressure that everyone wanted him to remain the same, to borrow words from John Lennon, "He just had to let it go!" Carl Jung would propose or postulate that César became the object of his own objectification. He grew up with parents subjected to injustices regarding financial issues surrounding the loss of their home and this was most impressionable on his early childhood; it became a symbolic example of social injustice left unexamined.

He struggled with feelings of identity knowing, like most people, that he did not possess the knowledge to help him do so; it caused consternation for César. Another way of putting this is that his deep feelings of identity shaped the manner in which he constructed his reality in everyday life. Yet his reasoning was superlative, often parallel with that found in the logic of the widely accepted Western idea of the scientific method and ingenuity. He had great feelings of confidence about who he was and what he stood for, creating an idealized self-image to strive and live for, while exuding sagacity. This brought meaning to his life.

People saw him as wise and charismatic and he internalized that perception early in his personal development. From a social psychological perspective, he came to see himself the way others saw him. He remained bothered by the fact that he was perceived as a charismatic figure by many, but lacked a solid education. You see this in people who become rich and famous but did not graduate from high school or attend college; they always wonder what they missed.

To some extent he sought refuge in the wisdom he was being credited for. Again, he showed many signs of scientific logic and was always in constant search of new questions that might help him reflect from a different perspective and gain insight into the meaning of his life. People close to him would say he "took on a bit of a mystique." It's true he did, but it was not fully of his own making; after all, when one takes on a pensive look people wonder what you are thinking about. This was certainly the case with César as Aldous Huxley puts it:

> *The mystic objectifies a rich feeling in the pit of the stomach into a cosmology.*
> —Aldous Huxley, *Chrome Yellow*, 1921.

César was no fool nor was he a mystic. He took the mystical into account, however, much as most scientists do. Simply a part of the scientific enterprise, at times it is, in fact, hard to ignore, especially when scientific discoveries are made by accident. Think about it this way: if you organized a march and invited one hundred and fifty people and over fifteen thousand people showed up in support of your vision, wouldn't you feel a little mystical about the experience? Psychologically, massive crowds of people have an intense impact on the psyche of individuals.

> *L'âme, prison du corps. (The soul is the prison of the body)*
> – Michel Foucault

To be sure, it was widely known that César felt strongly about the importance of education; he would say, "Knowledge is power." It was Sir Frances Bacon who popularized the notion that "power is knowledge," but Foucault would say that "knowledge is power," making the point that:

> *...at least for the study of human beings, the goals of power and the goals of knowledge cannot be separated: in knowing we control and in controlling we know.*

César deepened his understanding of this idea by reading the works of the philosopher Michel Foucault as he saw things in Foucault's thinking he could directly relate to. Two ideas that first attracted César to Foucault's thought were, "L'âme, prison du corps" or "the soul is the prison of the body" (see Foucault's only book on literature, *Death and the Labyrinth*, 1963) and also Foucault's idea that, "The game [life] is worthwhile insofar as we don't know what will be the end." César took these ideas to heart; fact is, he took ideas like these so personally that they began to transform him in such a way so as to make him noticeably more introspective and philosophical. Psychoanalytically speaking, you might say the outside social movement moved inward towards his soul and became a personal search for identity in the form of a mini social movement within his Self (in a social psychological sense).

He realized that in his leadership of the United Farm Workers, people knew (even if subliminally so), that he was actually leading a collective search for identity, but in César's heart and soul he knew first and foremost that he had first to find himself before he could continue to lead others. This thought remained ambiguous to him for the remainder of his life. This became his greatest internal struggle.

As shown in his organizing efforts, César, who had for so long professed the perils of individuality, was faced with new ideas that caused a cognitive shift so great in his thinking, personal philosophy and leadership that at times he became suspended existentially—caught in a web of contradictions. In order to ground César's philosophy, Fred Ross, who was the Organizing Director for the United Farm Workers throughout the 1960s, used to talk with César about collaborating with him on a "How to" manual for organizing movements and frankly this weighed heavily on his mind. So whether "knowledge is power" or "power is knowledge," César felt that he had to get something in writing, documenting their efforts in some form or another that would help future generations, but he was simply inundated with organizing activities and couldn't find the time.

While examining the relationship between power, scientific knowledge and domination, César came to an understanding of Foucault's paradigm. It's no wonder César became obsessed with how knowledge defines power and can become a tool for social control. By viewing the world of agribusiness in this way, education and domination became in his mind inseparable as described in Foucault's masterpiece, *Discipline and Punish* (1977). Foucault taught him the importance of possessing a paradigm for looking at everyday life, I recall César saying:

Armando A. Arias

Hijo de la frontera! Imagina su vida sin un paradigma para mirar, that is, "Son of the borderland! Imagine your life without a paradigm for looking."

At a time when César took the UFW's organizing efforts into full swing, he would often remark:

Persiguiendo a los placeres terrenales sólo conduce a la frustración, that is, "Chasing earthly pleasures only leads to frustration."

César wanted to experience enlightenment (especially as discussed by Foucault) as it was an idea that caught his imagination and he only became, "curiouser and curiouser." He had not been formally trained as an intellectual, but he was curious about everything, a drive that was innate in him. What he wanted most was to develop techniques for training the imagination; at times he became preoccupied with becoming enlightened. People from all walks of life such as Senator Robert Kennedy were pulling on his ear, introducing new ideas in hopes that they might provide support, energy, strength, and knowledge to his psyche.

At some point in his organizing, I believe it was Dr. Refugio Rochin, a professor at the University of California, Davis, and member of a Nobel Prize winning team, who introduced him to Foucault's thoughts and ideas (or maybe it was me) in which he found endless commonalities thinking that frankly were uncanny, from self-transformation to sympathy for oppressed peoples to ideas about social control and domination. César even began thinking about Foucault's theory of how architectural design impacts human behavior: comparing prisons to the layout of agricultural fields and how every worker is always in plain sight. It was by virtue of his very existence as a charismatic leader having experienced a life where many looked upon him as a saint that precipitated his transformation. César said:

Theorizing César Chávez

When people look at me like I am a saint, it changes the way I see the world, I even start to ask myself if I was born to be a saint...

Like scientists, César adapted a new attitude and ethos in his new-found philosophical tendencies, which allowed for unintentional outcomes of his external organizing activities in successfully championing a massive organizing movement. A statement by Foucault was found scribbled on note paper on César's side-table at the time of his death:

> *I don't feel that it is necessary to know exactly what I am. The main interest in life and work is to become someone else that you were not in the beginning.*

César was living and labor organizing during a time of high social protest against the War in Vietnam, protest against authority, sexual revolution, revolt on colleges campuses, the Beatles and John Lennon professing to "give peace a chance," the popularization of nude beaches and the advent of Black Power and the Chicano Movement, the spread of recreational drugs, the Cuban Missile Crisis, sending a man to the moon and the assassination of President John F. Kennedy and his brother Senator Robert Kennedy to whom he had grown very close, and of Martin Luther King, Jr. As a popular French philosopher, Michel Foucault was at the top of his game, producing an endless array of radical ideas; in his voice, we often heard his social analysis of the activities of the UFW, as if he were providing advice from his office at the University of California in Berkeley (1970s).

It's no wonder César began to tune in to Foucault's thinking. Knowing his personality, it was the best thing for him at the time, that is, wanting to examine his own being and reality. Becoming passionate for ontological study is common to people who rise to notoriety or fame unexpectedly and César came to have the desire to search for an inner truth while at the same time continuing to serve the UFW—this was the reason he was suspended existentially, caught in a web of contradictions; he grew to have that look of constant pensiveness. The search for inner truth won out; searching for his real being, his true Self, became a new passion, one he didn't see coming. He often stated, "Only by giving our lives, do we find life." This was César's mind-set at the time of his death.

Layer by layer, he began uncovering new things about himself. If he sometimes appeared subdued, he clearly was not; he was searching his soul trying to develop a clearer understanding of global issues (especially education, disease, climate change, development and social change). In this way, César began internalizing the passions and concerns of progressive minded intellectuals, well-educated people, smart politicos and everyone who wanted to see improvements in social justice and economic change in American society.

César was quite brave and willing to place himself at personal risk in pursuit of what he believed were higher goals for all people. When he began his search for his inner-truth, he found this to be a high calling and one that took, even by his own admission, more energy to be brave. He needed to be certain that his new existential plight was simply not an invention of his imagination, because he also wanted to make a real difference in addressing major global issues of the day.

SECTION 7 - CONCLUSION

Chapter Nineteen:

César's Sensibilities for Humanity and Mother Earth: Creating Presence in His Absence

Just prior to César's passing people everywhere began taking notice of weather changes and the popularity of global warming began to take hold. Perhaps even more than the phenomenon itself, what César found fascinating was how experts on the subject matter of global warming were often not taken seriously by non-experts; especially non-experts with power—politicos. Said differently, César realized that global warming had become so politicized that it changed the definition of what scientists (experts) report. For instance, a number of opinion polls have been taken about whether or not global warming exists and these polls are based mostly on the opinions of the average person on the street (non-experts). The people being polled are not scientists they were for the most part average people in retail jobs like those who work as baristas at coffee shops. The results of said polls were often pitted against the findings of years of scientific research conducted by climatologists and environmental scientists from around the world, yet in the court of popular opinion you could say the "baristas won out." What César came to realize was that "perception is everything" in American society and that was the truth.

In 2014, the GOP took over the House of Representatives, passed a law, H.R. 1422, that would:

Shake up the EPA's Scientific Advisory Board, placing restrictions on those pesky scientists and creating room for experts with overt financial ties to the industries affected by EPA regulations.

The passage of this law was interpreted by many professional scientists as a gag order hence they would no longer be able to report on their own research for fear of bias. Let me state this again: scientists who spent their entire lives researching a particular phenomenon (say the negative impact of pesticides on the human nervous system) are now with the passage of H.R. 1422 not allowed to present their research findings to the EPA's Scientific Advisory Board in favor of corporately hired researchers. (This is like not allowing a university professor to use his or her own best-selling peer-reviewed text-book in their own class because they make profits from book sales.) The point of the law was to include the input of industry experts which have historically been perceived as hired guns, and exclude the voice of professional scientists who spent their lives' conducting research on any particular field. Well?

César clearly saw this new law as an injustice. He argued that these are biased, politically driven polls, targeting non-experts whose opinions were being supported by industry experts hired to promote the interests of greedy corporate entities to include those who perform research on harmful pesticides. This worried César as he knew that various permutations of dangerous pesticides would never end. César fully understood how the political game was played and remained dismayed with what he called the "politics of science and the science of politics." It's no wonder why César found science and scientific inquiry so intriguing.

César found the scientific enterprise quite amusing. I only wish he were here to hear the news about how the European Space Agency (ESA) successfully landed a comet-chasing spacecraft named "Rosetta" on a comet called "Churyumov – Gerasimendo." In the spirit of theorizing César Chávez, I imagine his knee-jerk response in hearing the news for the first time would have been very close to this:

Now let me get this straight. Ten years ago the ESA sent a spacecraft named "Rosetta" into outer space to chase and catch up with a comet traveling 38,000 miles an hour that is more than 4 billion miles away. It circles the comet for 2 years at just 10 kilometers above its surface, starts to land on the surface of the comet, takes 2 reckless bounces and is demolished, is that so?

Contemplating this, César would enter into a pensive state, followed by a smile and a shake of his head, causing his smile to disappear and reappear moments later; it was like watching the wheels in his head turn. Anyone who knew him well would know that whatever he was thinking, whatever it was that was driving his smile up and down again, knew he was connecting ideas most people would consider far-fetched, a phenomenon the psychologist Carl Jung call "individuation." The point is that knowing César he was most likely thinking about how fascinating it was that scientists could follow the same methodologies as land-surveyors utilizing similar tools and measure the distance to a distant comet some four billion miles away yet farmers could not truly measure the size of their own property. To be sure not being able to truly measure the size of one's property was more than likely a political act as farmers liked to play the role of what they called the "boob." In playing the role of the "boob" they would say things that made them sound like they didn't really know much about farming or the size of their property and it was hoped that this would give them a home field advantage over say property tax assessors when they would report that they owned less than what appeared to be the case. Or, when the United Farm Workers began to organize farm workers in the fields farmers reported they owned more land than they did in order to rid themselves of trespassers and the local law enforcement always supported their definition of the boundaries they reported. Jokingly, César would most likely say something like they were "Rosetta- stoned."

Recall that it was César Chávez who during his organizing efforts in the agricultural fields called farm workers out of the fields while standing on the perimeters of the fields. Farmers came after César with loaded guns assuming their property lines went as far as the country roads contiguous with their property, but in most cases César had to remind them that county permits were issued with eminent domain and so the area between county roads and the agricultural fields was public property, and sure enough this is what caused César's smile all at once up-and-down again during pensive states, only to be tickled by the connection of new ideas once again. His mélange of abstraction surrounding farmer's perception of their own land held them suspended in their own thinking long enough for César to only devise more strategies to confuse them. In other words, he measured the intervals of both his ideas and language just enough to keep the farmers in abeyance.

Similarly, it was through his work that César came to know that up until the 1970s based on eminent domain the government had the right to expropriate private agricultural properties (with or without payment) as evidenced by thousands of strategically placed nuclear war-head missile silos placed on farms throughout the country. Surveyors in respective counties often ignored land-areas on the perimeters of agricultural land not for political reasons, but for practical ones, because it was simply a lot easier to measure the distances of property lines out to and/or up against country roads. It's no wonder that after generations of being farmers, they believed their property lines extended to the road. Due to this perception and while living in a society where "perception is everything" for the most part, farmers ignored the spirit of eminent domain and plowed through (pun intended) with their beliefs. It's no wonder the idea of surveyors not being able to accurately measure the size of one's agricultural field caught César's attention, yet by contrast astrophysicists are able to utilize tools similar to land-surveying instruments to accurately measure the distance to a moving comet or other universes billions of miles away; this tickled César in this way as did many other seemingly far-fetched ideas. This is an excellent example of why farmers and corporate lobbyists that attack them should be inclusive of the scientific findings made by professional scientists. Not only must scientist devise fool proof methodologies that can be replicated and tested by others, they must also present their findings publicly and this should rid their research of any built-in bias, something private researchers are not subjected to; besides, unlike land-surveyors, scientists, namely astrophysicists in this case can't measure on the side of wrong as they would miss the comet.

César would certainly add further rationale related to science policy in this country and say something like:

> *And so if under H.R. law 1422 scientists are not allowed to report their findings to the Scientific Advisory Board then we just increased our chances of being hit by an incoming asteroid a thousand times over as we (humanity and the earth) are nothing but a suspended target in a shooting gallery – thank you GOP!*

César's proclivity for individuation or seeing linkages between far-fetched ideas was more than just skepticism of modern science as well as agricultural science and was certainly well-founded especially when he made observations like this one (above) linking science and politics, he simply couldn't see it any other way.

The Rosetta spacecraft and its ability to successfully land on a moving comet was only possible through corroboration, something César dedicated his life to. César was all too aware of how corroboration needed to be paramount for all those involved in high-stake projects and this is what made him a charismatic leader as well as effective negotiator between the United Farm Workers (UFW) and farm workers. It goes back to his superlative logic. What he does know is that corroboration enables everyone involved to learn and provide new ideas. He also knew that at the same time conflict leads to new discoveries, new solutions and solutions to problems people don't often know they have; César had the uncanny ability to see problems coming. He would be more than dismayed to find that even today when astrophysicists are landing on a moving comet when science has come such a long way the austere living and working conditions experienced by farm workers continues to need much improvement—this is how he thought.

From a scientific research point of view, an early César Chávez would urge today's big ticket scientists to research not only the impact pesticides have on humans (the human nervous system) but on the environment as well, especially to include a focus on long-term impacts (i.e., the rising rates of asthma in older farm workers as well as the thinning of the uterus walls in young females and suicide rates of farmers). In other words, people could observe with their own eyes helicopters spraying pesticides directly onto farm workers toiling in the fields yet no one was up in arms about it: he saw this as slow and direct violence. For César the future was grim: pesticides became the analogy for all things toxic and he wanted more than anything to raise the flag of volatile urgency. "We are killing our Mother," he once said while in a pensive state when reflecting on the realities of pesticide use, global warming and today's climate calamity.

What César Would Say and What You Can Say About César

The César Chávez we last knew envisioned what Naomi Klein in her book, *This Changes Everything: Capitalism vs. the Climate* (Simon & Schuster, 2014) refers to as a "Marshal Plan for Earth." He wanted to help all of humanity in this way. César had a close relationship to Senator Robert Kennedy and met with President Kennedy on several occasions even during the threat of nuclear obliteration at the time of the Cuban Missile Crisis. César became focused on the idea that President Kennedy made clear in his 1961 address to the United Nations "Every inhabitant of this planet must contemplate the day when this planet may no longer be habitable." In César's mind it didn't make a difference as to what made the planet uninhabitable; his point was that whatever it (the threat) was we (humanity) had to act for concerted social change.

César would have been elated and found curious the technological and scientific advances discovered during the mission of the Rosetta spacecraft that chased a comet for ten years for over four billion miles and he would reflect about how this technology might also be used to improve upon the human condition of farm workers and the poor of the world. And in the much larger scheme of things, Rosetta would represent to him an effort to develop technology that could possibly save humanity either from itself or unknown future threats only his future recollection would know. It was this type of thinking he exuded that drew his attention to global warming and taking care of Gaia (Mother Earth) as it is a global issue that he felt strongly we should all care about. César did not see global warming as exclusively an environmental crisis as he also saw it as a cultural crisis, a "cultural Black Plague" as he once put it. These are but some of César's scientific sensibilities.

As a tool to make visible the peculiar nature of the scientific enterprise, the scientific method as well as the methods it is hoped that in this presentation of César's superlative logic as an alternate engagement of other ways of knowing STEM fields: science, technology, engineering and mathematics. Moreover, by viewing STEM fields through César's lens (taking into account his values and beliefs) we can develop creative infusions of ideas for us to take into account when unraveling the practice of science. Furthermore, in an attempt to advance a new paradigm for looking at STEM fields I have borrowed heavily from my own psychoanalysis of César Chávez as a scientific thinker and one who reflected heavily on how to empower people, keep them safe, improve upon their human condition and provide them with solutions to problems they didn't know they had. This insight became the driving force behind why it is he took a broad philosophical stance in the public eye to support all peoples experiencing injustices in this and other countries. And because that was so, César:

- Would encourage us to be more invitational to others and to be open-minded to the scientific cultural ways of others; he was always very inclusive.

- Was a proponent of the need to use scientific studies to demonstrate that certain technological advances were demonstrably bad for the agricultural working-class. He hated the use of pesticides such as DDTs and Methol bromide on farm workers while they toiled in the fields.

- Didn't approve of the research on gene splicing; he would say "There's something inherently wrong with genetically altering the food we eat."

- Would say, "A real STEM education must take into account the 'marriage' between the arts, humanities, social & behavioral and natural (hard) sciences. Si se puede!"

- Wanted to expand literacy because he wanted people to understand the perils of technological advances like gene splicing.

- Was also in favor of spreading the word to all sectors in society about who produced their food.

- Had heart related problems that promoted his need to eat healthily and was adverse to the consumption of genetically altered crops and farm products, like meat and milk-based products.

- Was all for building a gender free view of science or an integrated male-female paradigm for solving scientific issues and scientific problems.

- Would offer the following: "When it comes to examining the fields found in the STEM program, it's not about how each field can stand alone; it's more about creating an integrative vision infusing all of the sciences and in this way it is not about the respective sciences. It's about the people."

In this sense, he was an advocate for political and social change within STEM fields and all sciences.

Theorizing César Chávez

To tell the story of César Chávez' life in this manner is at the same time intellectually pragmatic as well as existential as his head was deeply rooted in his heart and his thoughts, ideas and sensibilities. In keeping his spirit alive and in creating a presence in his absence take these ideas into account. César Chávez:

- Was very approachable; he always wanted to talk, he especially enjoyed one-on-one conversations. César was a known empathic listener (a characteristic hard to find in leaders these days).

- Would visit and interview farmworkers in their homes and sometimes in the agricultural fields and inquire about their austere living and working conditions.

- Was a labor organizer and this shaped who he was and what he stood for.

- Gained insight by listening to farmworkers and came up with solutions to individual and group problems, in turn this gave farmworkers confidence to band together and cause change; this became known as "La Causa." His ideals gave many in the Chicano and other movements an optimism they didn't have before; in this way he helped spearhead global movements towards social change.

- Was able to take the struggle of the farmworker's and plant it squarely in the American psyche by bringing to light not only the austere working conditions experienced by farmworkers but also how they were often exploited through threats of deportation.

- Played a role in thwarting a nuclear holocaust during the Cuban Missile Crisis and following his influential role, Nikita Khrushchev, the premier of the once Soviet Union, offered César Chávez a full scholarship (through the Ph.D.)

to study a topic of choice in the academic town of Akademgorodok (Soviet Union).

- Became interested in organic farming (biodynamic agriculture) and raised global awareness about the negative impact pesticides had on people and the environment.

- Entered into a personal transformational stage that many recognized but did not decipher; amongst his most significant others, it became the unspeakable truth.

- Was admired by many throughout the world for his idealism and was perceived as a charismatic leader.

- Possessed an insatiable curiosity for the nature of science its theories and methods. The national STEM movement led him to ask, "STEM for whom?"

- Had a superlative logic and uncanny ability to see situations quite differently than most and was good at thinking outside-of-the-box.

- Was a warm, sincere person and nice to be around.

Lastly, in the words of César Chávez, "We can cause social change only when we change ourselves!"

AFTERWORD

César Chávez and the Development of the Chicano Scientific Psyche

Think about your personal Chicano/a perspective (ideas, personal ideology, worldview as well as your feelings) and how your reality is constructed in daily life. Also, think about how your political consciousness was developed, where it came from and why you have the ideas and perspectives you do, especially about such things as the use of pesticides (Methyl bromide) on farmworkers while they toil in the fields or how it is that pesticides are causing more and more miscarriages in young Latinas due to the thinning of the uterus walls. A direct correlation exists between the rising rates of cancer in children who live in agricultural regions and the use of harmful pesticides.

Yet, while this is a widely known fact, it doesn't seem to be alarming to the American populace; people enjoy fresh fruits and vegetables, but they don't want to know how they were produced. The same goes for the increased presence of chlorofluorocarbons (CFCs) produced every day from car emissions while waiting to cross the U.S.-Mexico Port of Entry at Tijuana-San Diego. CFCs are a form of pesticide that causes cancer and kills everything on earth.

César Chávez used to point out that in the "name of science" the focus is on how to perform research on how to gene splice the make-up of a tomato in order that a machine may pick it or it grow at a faster rate rather than researching the welfare of the people picking the tomatoes. For César Chávez, it was a contradiction that shaped his worldview or his paradigm for critically examining the agricultural industry. But his observations didn't stop there; he directly observed thousands of farm workers living in miserable living conditions, paying high rent for dilapidated housing, often without running water or toilets that worked. He saw farm workers without health benefits, fair wages and worker's rights and he introduced these conditions to the world.

Turning César's logic back on itself is the key to our insight, so in the "name of science" we need not only to encourage our youth to pursue STEM (science, technology, engineering and mathematics) fields of study; we also need for them to focus on the sciences that will improve upon the human condition. Had César come to know drones, he would have observed that their use should be changed from firing missiles to delivering medicine or goods to farm workers in rural areas throughout the world.

César's ideas, values and beliefs caused what the philosopher Nietzsche calls a "transvaluation of values" in millions of people. In short, he caused what they refer to in science as a paradigm shift in our view of the world, of having gone from one set of values that didn't fully recognize injustices to a set of values that do—this is the essence of Chicanismo.

In all the talk about "What is a Chicano?" this is the realization that César's values have had on the Latino psyche. We think about what César brings to our attention and it suspends our own personal experiences and causes us to reinterpret them through a new critical lens. This then is the premise in this work, revealing to some extent realities in STEM fields that are unjust and/or unforeseen.

César's ideas are as "Alberto" Einstein put it when referring to the importance of explaining scientific ideas, such as his theory of relativity, "Keep it simple, but not too simple." César's logic is a lot like the science of particle physicists, but instead he might refer to it as the "theory of relatives and humanity" (said tongue-in-cheek, of course). First, we start out with a basic idea, such as, which particle (in physics terms) is responsible for the beginning of our world. What we have heard or learned is what scientists call the "Big Bang." That's the big or simple side of the question, and as César would suggest, we peel back the layers in search of what we are calling the "god-particle."

What we find is that we move from the gross or atomic level to endless subatomic levels, each time moving to a new level of understanding not realized before discovering the unforeseen. We can refer to this as the "not-so-simple" level of understanding, which is of course the essence of the scientific method. César performed the same sort of deconstructing logic when in his surface level observations, he would say "farmworkers are being mistreated in the fields and live in dire conditions." He then looks a little deeper and finds that many times farmworkers don't even get paid and are forced to live in dilapidated conditions paying high rent; he peels back more layers of reality and discovers:

> *It's not about the lettuce or grapes, it's about the people.*

Much like Einstein, César says so much with so few words, he has the logical ability to deconstruct human behavior in a manner that "keeps it simple but not too simple," he intensifies the obvious, he restates what we already "see." We just can't see the obvious because in American society "perception is everything" and we more often than not prefer to live the illusion (perception) and this becomes César's point of logical departure. César's contrasting constructions of reality can at the same time appear trivial. "It's not about the lettuce or grapes," but also profound, "it's about the people."

My home is in the great Salinas Valley located next to thousands of acres of agricultural fields. I see farmworkers toiling in the fields, working, bending over, carrying heavy pipes, always moving quickly as many are paid by the crate, all the while the crop dusters spray pesticides over each and every one of them and over me as well. I teach their children in my classes and they teach me, and I can't help but think about the dehumanizing effect technological "advances" are having in our own backyard only to increase the margins of the agricultural industries $8.3 billion annual profit (in the Salinas Valley alone) to better exploit them as well as all other peoples subjected to labor conditions of a similar sort. I seek refuge in what César always stressed in the inclusion of all people:

> *Our ambitions must be broad enough to include the aspirations and needs of others, for their sakes and for our own.*

César was a huge environmentalist; he was always worried about Mother Nature and was especially concerned about the long-lasting effects of pesticides not only on people but also on the land. And now that the U.S. Geological Society has confirmed perhaps the largest deposits of oil ever discovered in the form of shale-oil (used as a substitute for crude oil) lie beneath the great Salinas Valley (an estimated trillion gallons), an agricultural area so vast it can be spotted as a massive green spot from outer space, the entire industry could be at stake in the very near future. The short of it is that we may very well be exchanging green vegetables for "greenbacks," U.S. dollars, and the only way you can see "green backs" from outer space is if you turn the Salinas Valley into Dubai; it could happen in our lifetime. What would César say about this? Hijole!

Everywhere I look I see a paradigm for looking at daily life as would César Chávez, multi-perspectivally and multi-dimensionally as well. César thought "out-of-the-box" to be sure and he had an impact on others to do the same, still does. It's very much like César says:

> *Once social change begins, it cannot be reversed. You cannot uneducate the person who has learned to read. You cannot humiliate the person who feels pride. You cannot oppress the people who are not afraid anymore.*

César communicated ideas and instilled them in people in a way that demystified realities that are found in situations in the agricultural fields and in so doing applied his rational inquiry making situations less frightening. César's philosophy of everyday life was ontological to be sure as he pondered the very existence of all humanity and how it might be improved through scientific breakthroughs with technology but without exploitation.

BIBLIOGRAPHY

Avineri, Shlomo (2019). *Karl Marx: Philosophy and Revolution.* New Haven, Connecticut: Yale University Press.

Beer, Stafford (1995). *Viable Systems Models (VSM).* Cavendish Software Ltd.

Benjamin, Arthur (2015). *The Magic of Math: Solving for x and Figuring Out Why.* New York, New York: Basic Books.

Blow, Charles (2014, December 10). *This is Your Moment.* New York Times (The Opinion Pages).

Bruno, Leonard & Lawrence Baker (1999). *Math and Mathematicians: The History of Math Discoveries Around the World.* Detroit, Mich.: UXL.

Busch, Akiko (2005). *The Uncommon Life of Common Objects: Essays on Design and the Everyday.* Los Angeles, CA: Metropolis Book Publishing Press.

Camus, Albert (2016). *The Stranger.* New York, New York: Vintage Books.

Caplan, Caralee E. (1992, April 8). Chavez urges fruit boycott, attacks growers, politicians for not banning pesticides. *Harvard Crimson.*

Chávez, C. (1984, November 9). Address to the Commonwealth Club of California.

CREATE - Center for Research on Educational Equity, Assessment and Teaching Excellence (2020). University of California, San Diego: San Diego, CA.

Csíkszentmihályi, Mihály (2009). *Flow: The Psychology of Optimal Experience.* New York, New York: Harper Collins.

de Tocqueville, Alexis/ Richard D. Heffner (ed.) (1863/2001). *Democracy in America.* New York, NY: New American Library. (Penguin Group).

Descartes, René (1637). *Discourse of the Method of Rightly Conducting One's Reason and of Seeking Truth in the Sciences.* London, England: Orion Publishing Group.

DeVol, R. (2018, September). *"How do research universities contribute to regional economies? Measuring research university contributions to regional economies."* Arkansas: Walmart Family Foundation.

Einstein, A. (1920). *Relativity: The Special and General Theory.* (Digital reprint).

Federation of Enterprise Architect Professional Organizations (2013, November Issue 9-4). *Common Perspective on Enterprise Architecture.* Architecture and Governance Magazine.

Feyerabend, Paul (1987). *Farewell to Reason.* Brooklyn, New York: Verson Books.

Feyerabend, Paul (1982). *Science in a Free Society.* New York: Verson Books.

Foucault, Michel (2012). *Discipline and Punishment: The Birth of the Prison.* New York: Vintage Books.

Foucault, Michel (1963). *Death and the Labyrinth.* Wiltshire: Cromwell Press.

Foucault, Michel (1969). *L'archéologie du savoir (in French).* The Archaeology of Knowledge. Paris: Gallimard.

Freud, Sigmund (1930). *Civilization and Its Discontents.* London, England: Penguin.

Gooding, David (1989). *History in the Laboratory: The Development of the Laboratory.* London: Macmillan.

Griswold del Castillo, Richard (2008). *César Chávez: The Struggle for Justice / César Chávez: La lucha por la justici*a (English and Spanish Edition). Anthony Accardo (Illustrator). Houston: Piñata Press.

Griswold del Castillo, Richard and Garcia, Richard A. (1995). *César Chávez: A triumph of spirit.* Norman, OK: University of Oklahoma Press.

Hayes-Bautista, David (2017). *La Nueva California: Latinos from Pioneers to Post – Millennials.* Berkeley, CA: The University of California Press.

Heintz, Christophe. (2012). *Scaffolding on Core Cognition. In: Developing Scaffolds in Evolution, Culture and Cognition.* Edited by: Linda R. Caporael, James Griesemer, William C. Wimsatt. Boston, Mass: MIT Press.

Heintz, Christophe. (2002). *Can mathematical meaning allow cultural analysis? In: Travelling Concepts II: Frame, Meaning, and Metaphor.* Edited by: J. Goggin, J. Loontjes. Amsterdam: ASCA Press.

Huerta, Dolores (2008). *A Dolores Huerta Reader.* Albuquerque, NM: University of New Mexico Press.

Huerta, Dolores (2008). *A Dolores Huerta Reader.* Albuquerque, NM: University of New Mexico Press.

Huxley, Aldous (1932). *Brave New World.* New York: Rosetta Books.

Huxley, Aldous (1932). *Chrome Yellow.* United Kingdom: Chatto & Windus.

James, William (1912). *Essays in Radical Empiricism.* Paternoster, London: Longmans, Green, and Co.

Jardine, Lisa & Michael Silverthorne (2000). *Francis Bacon: The New Organon.* Cambridge, United Kingdom: Cambridge University Press.

Johnson, Gaye Theresa (2013), *Spaces of Conflict, Sounds of Solidarity: Music, Race, and Spatial Entitlement in Los Angeles.* Berkeley, CA: University of California Press.

Jung, Carl (1921). *Psychological Types.* Verlag, Zurich: Rascher Verlag.

Klein, Naomi (2014). *This Changes Everything: Capitalism vs. the Climate.* New York, NY: Simon & Schuster.

Kuhn, Thomas (1962/1970). *The Structure of Scientific Revolutions.* Chicago: University of Chicago Press (2nd edition, with postscript).

Kuhn, Thomas (1959). "The Essential Tension: Tradition and innovation in Scientific Research," in *The Third University of Utah Research Conference on the Identification of Scientific Talent.* C. W. Taylor, ed. Salt Lake City: University of Utah Press, 162–74.

Le Bon, Gustav (1895/2018). *The Crowd: A Study of the Popular Mind.* Minneapolis, Minnesota: SMK Books.

Lederman, Leon (1993). *The God Particle: If the Universe Is the Answer, What Is the Question?* New York, NY: Dell Publishing.

Lovelock, James (2006). "Past the Tipping Point and the Fate of Humanity." Address to world-class scientists at the Big Sur Environmental Institute, Big Sur, CA.

Mannheim, Karl (1949). *Ideology and Utopia.* New York, NY: Harcourt Brace.

Marcuse, Herbert (1964). *One-Dimensional Man: Studies in the Ideology of Advanced Industrial Society.* Boston: Beacon Press.

Meier, Sid. *Alpha Centauri: The Future of Mankind*. 4X video game by Fraxis Games.

Merleau-Ponty, M. (1964). *Le visible et l'invisible*, Paris: Gallimard; *The visible and the invisible*, Alphonso Lingis (trans.), Evanston: Northwestern University Press.

Miller, A. C. (1995, May 30). *FBI spied on Cesar Chavez for years, files reveal*. Los Angeles Times.

Nietzsche, Friedrich (1887). *On the Genealogy of Morality: A Polemic*. Verlag, Leipzig.

Orwell, George (1949). *1984*. London, England: Secker & Warburg.

Pawel, Miriam. (2014). *The Crusades of César Chávez: A Biography*. New York: Bloomsbury Press.

Piaget, Jean (1971). *Structuralism*. New York, NY: Routledge & Kegan Paul.

Plato (2018 Reprint of 1875 Second Edition). *The Allegory of the Cave*. New York, NY: Barnes & Noble Press Publishing.

Plato (First published in England, 1871). *The Republic*. London, England: Pantianos Classics.

Powell, W. (1971). *The Anarchist Cookbook*. Arkansas: Ozark Press.

Rao, Prakash and Ann Reedy and Beryl Bellman (2010). "The Contribution of Enterprise Architecture to the Achievement of Organizational Goals: Establishing the Enterprise Architecture Benefits Framework," Technical Report, Department of Information and Computing Sciences, Utrecht University, Utrecht, The Netherlands, (online).

Rogers, Carl (1961). *On Becoming a Person: A Therapist's View of Psychotherapy*. Boston: MA.

Rogers, Carl (1995). *A Way of Being*. Boston, MA: Houghton Mifflin Harcourt Company.

Ross, Fred (1989). *Conquering Goliath: Cesar Chavez at the Beginning*. El Taller Graphico Press.

Stokes, Phillip (2012). *Philosophy: 100 Essential Thinkers: The Ideas That Have Shaped Our World*. London, England: Arcturus Publishing Limited.

Tweney, Ryan D. (2004). *"Replication and the Experimental Ethnography of Science," Journal of Cognition and Culture (4.3, 2004)*.

Weber, Max. (1905). *The Protestant Ethic and the Spirit of Capitalism*. Vigeo Press.

Wittgenstein, Ludwig (1922). *Tractatus Logico – Philosophicus*. New York, NY: Harcourt, Brace & Company.

Wodehouse, P. G. (1982). *Tales from the Drones Club*. Richmond, United Kingdom: Setanta Books.

Zinn, Howard (1980/2005). *A People's History of the United States*. New York, NY: Harper Perennial Modern Classics.

Theorizing César Chávez

"¡Si se puede!"

Made in the USA
Middletown, DE
24 October 2020